THE PRIMARY SCHOOL
NATIONAL CURRICULUM TOPIC BOOK

by

Peter Bell

with contributions by:

Janet Adams
Adrienne Dawes
Joanne Duckworth
Paul Duckworth
Dianne Williams

Published by:

"TOPICAL RESOURCES"

A DEFINITION OF THEMATIC WORK

Some people call it "Project Work". Some people call it "Topic" or "Centre of Interest" or "Environmental Studies". All of these terms it would seem refer to much the same sort of activity. Thematic work is an approach to teaching in a primary school which involves various often unrelated tasks being carried out under the umbrella of a common title or "Theme" such as "Ourselves", "Pets" or "Life in the Middle ages".

Thematic work always :
- (i) Crosses curriculum boundaries.
- (ii) Involves practical activities.
- (iii) Uses themes selected which are thought appropriate to the interests and stage of development of children involved.
- (iv) Involves first hand experiences such as visits or visitors.
- (v) Involves some sort of investigation.
- (vi) Involves information gathering skills.
- (vii) Includes class, group and individual work with some elements of choice.

It should also include, if possible, an element of "FUN"!!!

The Primary School National Curriculum Topic Book is available from all good Educational Bookshops and by mail order from:

TOPICAL RESOURCES,
P.O. BOX 329,
BROUGHTON,
PRESTON,
LANCASHIRE
PR3 5LT

Topical Resources publishes a range of Educational Materials for use in Primary Schools and Pre-School Nurseries and Playgroups.

FOR LATEST CATALOGUE Tel/Fax 01772 863158

Copyright © 1995 Peter Bell

Material from the National Curriculum is Crown copyright and is reproduced by permission of the Controller of HMSO

Printed in Great Britain for "Topical Resources" , Publishers of Educational Materials, P.O. Box 329, Broughton, Preston, Lancashire PR3 5LT (Telephone or fax 01772 863158), by T.Snape & Company Limited, Boltons Court, Preston, Lancashire.

Typeset by Janet Nielsen and Tracy Neale, White Cross Business Support Service, White Cross, South Road, Lancaster LA1 4XQ

First Edition Published October 1995.

ISBN 1 872977 10 3

INTRODUCTION

"If to plan one topic well is difficult, to organise a programme of topics succesfully is almost a miracle".

The purpose of this book is to provide a simple "whole primary school" framework using Themes and Topics to help deliver the Dearing version of the National Curriculum. The book covers the programmes of study in Science, Technology, History and Geography with suggestions for an approach to teaching R.E. The framework is intended to run parallel to existing schemes for the development of Language and Mathematics and will overlap with such schemes from time to time.

"The main area of weakness is in topic work. In common with this type of work in the country at large, teachers leave too much to chance in their planning and are unclear about their objectives and the opportunities for learning that need to be exploited. As a result the work is often over-prescribed, undemanding and lacking rigour."

Times Educational Supplement 19/2/88 reporting the chief H.M.I. Mr Eric Bolton's report on the performance of I.L.E.A.

Thematic work is often criticised in the Educational Press for its lack of rigour. Many people believe that it is a product of the sixties, endorsed by the Plowden Report, which will fail miserably due to the introduction of the National Curriculum. The approach does in fact go back much further than that. This book will trace out its ancestry, tease out its constituent parts and explore the types of themes which can be developed in a primary school.

"The approach can, in skilled hands, produce work of high quality. There is evidence to suggest that some schools, recognising the problems outlined above, are planning carefully structured topic frameworks for Years 1 to 6 which map the attainment targets and programmes of study of the subjects involved."

"The subject-focused topic, in particular, offers an efficient way forward."

Curriculum Organisation and Classroom Practice in Primary Schools- A discussion paper (1992) - Alexander, Rose and Woodhead.

Six years into the National Curriculum the topic approach is not only surviving but appears to be as popular as ever.

CONTENTS

A BRIEF HISTORY OF THEMATIC WORK

The poet, Laurie Lee, describes the boredom and disenchantment of his school days as having only one aim,

> to keep us out of the air and from following the normal pursuits of the fields... Crabby's science of dates and sums and writing seemed a typical invention of her own... prison labour like picking oakum or sewing sacks. (1)

The so called "progressive movement" grew up in direct contrast to exposition and demonstration, generally called class teaching. Rousseau (1712 - 1728), was one of the first exponents of activity methods and favoured a highly individualised form of education. He wrote:

> Teach your scholar to observe the phenomena of nature; you will soon rouse his curiosity, but if you would have it grow, do not be in too great a hurry to satisfy this curiosity. Put the problems before him and let him solve them himself... let him not be taught... let him discover.(2)

Froebel (1782 - 1852) considered that the best growth occurred through varied and contrasting activities which it was the job of the educationalists to provide. His belief in activity, expressive work and the use of constructional equipment for learning was intended to penetrate all stages of education. Instead they became an essential part of the education of nursery and infant children. Possibly "Payment by Results" was partly responsible for this as infants were literally those children below Standard 1 where children first encountered examinations.

The use of constructional equipment and sense training with the Infant age group was given further impact through the work of Maria Montessori (1870 - 1952).

At the turn of the century the ideas of John Dewey (1859 - 1952) began to influence the education of older children in the United States. He defined stages of problem-solving and suggested these as the main vehicles for learning in school. His approach led him to conclude that the whole of education could be implemented through cookery, textile making and workshop activities.

In his book "Foundation of Method" published in 1930, W.H.Kilpatrick modified Dewey's Problem Method into the Project Method. The emphasis here was on research, enquiry and discovery. He formulated four phases for the successful project: "purposing planning - executing - judging". Again this approach was a means of involving children in purposeful activity as a learning experience.

It was to the United States that the Hadow Committee turned for information on projects. The 1931 Hadow Report on "The Primary School", which was now in theory at least, separate from the Secondary School, suggested that the curriculum should be seen in terms of "activity and experience rather than knowledge to be acquired and facts to be stored". Teachers were asked to reconsider the teaching of separate subjects in distinct lessons. However, due to a concern for the maintenance of standards, teachers were encouraged to provide an adequate amount of "drill" in reading, writing and arithmetic. Concern about mixed ability recommended that where possible, children should be streamed. Possibly this was due to preparation for the "eleven-plus" examination!

The 1933 Hadow Report on Infant and Nursery Schools was less guarded. Learning was to be individualised. Knowledge to be acquired was to derive " not so much from an instruction, as from an instructive environment". Children were to spend a large part of their school day out of doors. Learning was to be through play. Freedom was said to be essential. The child was to learn the "three Rs" only when he wanted to, "whether he be three or six years of age". (4)

In 1947 Daniel's book "Activity in the Primary School" was published and this introduced activity methods at least to the lower ends of some Junior Schools.

In 1966 the Plowden Report suggested that "Finding out has proved to be better for children than being told", (5) but it could be argued the report did not suggest a curriculum totally run along these lines.

> We endorse the trend towards individual and active learning and "learning by acquaintance" and should like many more schools to be more deeply influenced by it. Yet we certainly do not deny the value of "learning by description" or the need for practice of skills and consolidation of knowledge. (6)

The Committee also recognised the problems individualised teaching would present in a class of over thirty pupils and for economy's sake suggested that a small group of children who are roughly at the same stage might be taught together.

In 1975 William Tyndale became a by-word for all that could go wrong with modern teaching methods and it is to be noted with interest thirteen years later the T.E.S. dated 11.3.88 H.M.I. comments on the same school:

> High standards, excellent work, industry and enjoyment. This is William Tyndale primary school in the 1980's...

> The school is less successful in mathematics and topic work, which includes history, Geography and Religious Education. (7)

The topic approach is certainly not without its problems. The use of terms such as Projects, Theme, Topic, Centre of Interest, Environmental Studies, etc. has caused much confusion over what project work is and how it can be recognised. This was clearly demonstrated when Leith (8) in 1978-9 asked thirty teachers to complete an assessment sheet which needed a clear understanding of and commitment to Kilpatrick's first principles of the approach. After two terms not one had used the procedure!

The Inspectorate paid little attention to the extent of project work in their 1978 survey report. R.E., History and Geography were said to be generally taught through topics such as "helping others" or "homes". The survey itself could well be at fault here as the teacher's questionnaire on the curriculum listed only traditional separate subjects with no mention of projects. The comments it did make were not particularly encouraging:

> Taken as a whole in four out of five of all the classes which studied History the work was superficial . In many cases it involved little more than copying from reference books and often the themes chosen had very little historical content. (9)

> Similar topics, for example, "homes", or "life on the farm" or "children of other lands" tended to appear in classes of all ages. This practice can lead to unnecessary repetition unless considerable care is taken to ensure there is progression in the work which children do. (10)

In addition to the problems many teachers appear to have had in putting the approach into practice lies the government's and the Inspectorate's remarkably consistent view of the curriculum as separate subjects. This is demonstrated in their many publications on the curriculum and in much of the work by the Schools Council.

Remarkably, many teachers still appear to be committed to the project approach. Henry Pluckrose (1987) writes in his book "What is Happening in our Primary Schools" about his time as a headteacher:

> After being taken round by a six or seven year old, parents visiting the school for the first time were given the opportunity to talk to me or to one of my colleagues. The discussions rarely centred upon how quickly John or Sandra might master mathematics or reading.

> These elements of the school programme would, it was assumed, somehow "come". What was demanded of me, however, was that school would provide a secure, happy environment in which children would have an opportunity to share ideas, to develop their social skills and to discover their particular individual gifts. (11)

He defends accusations that this sounds impossible and suggests opportunities must be given for children to talk through their ideas; talk which stems from experience. He argues the primary school should:

> provide a place where children can meet and talk with adults who live in and serve the local community - the fireman, the nurse, the secretary, the shopkeeper, the police officer, the craftsman and craftswoman. ...Such experiences vivify learning and give children the opportunity to talk and, through talk, to explore ideas ... Learning through first-hand experience provides the framework into which information obtained in other ways (from books, television and radio) can be fitted. (12)

The project approach is certainly able to provide opportunities for learning through first hand experience. As we move into the 1990's and the advent of the National Curriculum the whole debate about what teachers should teach and when has been taken out of their hands. This must change the emphasis from "what should I teach next" to "how am I going to teach this" and some of the many practicalities of implementing a successful whole school project approach may be solved. If this is the case, the 1990's could see the fulfilment of the educational promise of the 1960's

References

(1)   Cider with Rosie by Laurie Lee (1962) - Crabby was his teacher.

(2)   Emile by J.J. Rousseau (1762), P. 131.

(3)   Board of Education (1933) Infant to Nursery Schools, P.141.

(4)   Ibid, P. 133.

(5) Children and their Primary Schools - A report of the Central Advisory Council for Education (England) 1966, P460.

(6) Ibid, P.202.

(7) T.E.S. (11 .3.88), P.6.

(8) "Project Work: an EnigmaU, S. Leith (1981) in Simon & Wilcocks (eds.) (1981) Research and Practice in the Primary Classroom.

(9) Primary Education in England - A survey by H.M. Inspectors of Schools (1978),P.73.

(10) Ibid, P.74.

(11) What is Happening in our Primary Schools, H. Pluckrose (1987), P.3.

(12) Ibid, P.6.

THE THEORY

You would not attempt to teach an 18 year old "A" level student in the same way as a first year pupil in a secondary school (an age difference of seven years). Similarly, you would not attempt to teach a 4 year old reception pupil in the same way as a child in Primary Year 6, (again an age difference of seven years). Consequently, the same type of Theme or Topic approach cannot be applied to all ages in a Primary School.

This section of the book will consider the factors teachers need to take into account whilst planning Themes or Topics which progress from Reception to Year 6 in the Primary School.

The first factor to be dealt with is the importance of skills and concepts.

The Importance of Skills and Concepts

Why are skills and concepts important when planning thematic work? The Schools Council Project "Place, Time and Society" had this to say about information in today's world.

> History, Geography and the social sciences are often treated as information subjects in a world in which there is an information explosion. Today's fact maybe tomorrow's fallacy. When change is the norm there is a need to provide a framework both for teachers and for children which can help them to cope with change. (13)

Skills and concepts can provide such a framework. Jerome Bruner in the early sixties argued that instruction should be focussed on developing key concepts. He saw such concepts as opening doors to the understanding of the major disciplines and facilitating further learning. Once a child had some grasp of a key concept, other newly learned material could be related to it. As well as this, Bruner and others have identified in the disciplines characteristic methods of inquiry, or skills, which could also be learned and applied to new situations. Gunning, Gunning and Wilson argue that skills and concepts must go together.

> Having acquired a concept a child needs to use it...
> "skills can hardly be practised in a vacuum".....
> "learning skills and concepts are therefore complementary activities and should go hand in hand." (14)

An examination will now be made of the nature of skills and concepts in relation to thematic work.

Skills

According to Science in the Secondary School Curriculum a skill is:

> the ability to perform a task, whether manual or mental, which in turn involves working out and building up a series of processes and actions into a co-ordinated sequence to be followed. A skill can be learned by repeated experience of the sequence of processes and actions making up the skill, through which understanding is gained. (15)

In a primary school there are many skills to be learned. Essential to the author's definition of thematic work is the learning of basic study or information skills which will enable the child to extract information from various written and pictorial sources. Such skills will include:

(i)   Observation
      e.g. of objects, pictures, books, filmstrips, slides, maps, the environment, etc

(ii) Referencing
      e.g. using an index, contents page encyclopaedia, reference section in a library, etc.

(iii) Oral Communication
      e.g. listen, follow instructions, describe observations, recount and discuss experiences.

(iv) Recording
      e.g. present neat, well organised written work, use tables, charts, diagrams, graphs, drawings and models to supplement written work.

(v) Interpreting Information
   e.g. from maps, plans, diagrams tables, charts, etc. Analyse information at a simple level and draw conclusions.
(vi) Predicting and Hypothesising
   e.g. make simple predictions, attempt to explain causes and effects and plan the next stage in own research.

In addition to the learning of study skills common to many fields of enquiry will be the learning of various modes of enquiry that are specific to individual disciplines. Henry Pluckrose writes:

> The method we adopt to arrive at an answer will be peculiar to the enquiry (or discipline) we are exploring. (16)

Examples of these "specific" skills are: using evidence when researching History; map making in Geography; observation and identification in Nature Work; experimenting in practical Science; and the use of empathy in Religious Education.

David Wray (17) argues that if a project is seen as a means of teaching information skills then finding and handling particular sources of information will be a central feature of the work. Similarly, if we are teaching skills of using evidence or experimenting, then these skills too should be central features of the work. Hence using information skills and subject specific skills in an appropriate context should be part of the pupil activities to be considered when planning new thematic work.

Concepts

According to Science in the Secondary School Curriculum a concept is:

> an idea under the heading of which knowledge and experience can be classified and better understood. Related items of knowledge can, therefore, be grouped together under the heading of a broad concept such as energy or a more limited concept such as heat. (18)

Together with other educationalists, Piaget and Bruner are convinced of the central importance of conceptional development in the process of intellectual growth. They suggest that success in school subjects depends substantially on conceptional development and that it is not enough to leave this to chance.

Gunning, Gunning and Wilson state that "many concrete experiences contribute to the formation of these concepts". (19), but how do we choose appropriate concrete experiences when planning our thematic work.

A clue comes from Bruner's "Key" concepts. He suggests a subject is assumed to have certain characteristic or "Key" concepts which help towards the further understanding of the discipline. These "Key" concepts are what make some knowledge and experience for example come under the heading "History" and other knowledge and experience for example under the heading "Science".

Examples of "Key" Historical concepts could be:
   Past and Present.
   Continuity and Change.
   Sense of Chronology.
   Cause and Consequence.

Examples of "Key" Scientific concepts could be:
   Energy
   Materials
   Environment
   Alive and Dead

Inseparable from the idea of key concepts is that of Bruner's spiral curriculum. I quote:

> "children will first encounter key ideas and concepts in a primitive form in early childhood, and will re-encounter them in a more highly developed forms in their subsequent work in schools, each encounter leading to a more sophisticated understanding." (20)

Hence in our planning of thematic work it must be ensured "Key" concepts of the disciplines are introduced using concrete experiences at an early stage so that these concepts can be built upon using progressively more sophisticated experiences on a regular basis.

Bruner claims that his approach to teaching the concepts and skills which characterize a discipline means that "the foundations of any subject can be taught to anybody at any age in an intellectually respectable form". (21)

A teacher's goals must therefore be to develop the skills and concepts appropriate to the pupil's stage of development through a content of interest to the age group.

The Nature of the "Young Child" and His Work

What is a young child in a Primary School? English legislation states that a child must attend school full time during the school term following his/her fifth birthday.

Practice varies throughout the country with many local education authorities admitting children before they are five years old. From September 1987 Lancashire's policy has been to admit children to primary school in the September of the academic year the child is five years old. This means that the youngest primary children are barely four years old!

What is the "nature" of such a child? A quote from a reception class teacher in "Starting School: An Evaluation of the Experience" gives a clue to some of the needs that must be catered for.

> I really don't think teachers who have never taken reception classes appreciate the problems. They think you are just there to supervise them. They don't really realize the problems that you have to cope with as well as teaching them basic things. (22)

The report goes on to identify "survival skills" children need to learn, know and use in order to function confidently in the classroom. They include often assumed skills such as knowing who they are, what they can do and how to cope with and overcome "not knowing" things and the feelings this arouses. Six other skills were also listed.

An L.E.A. Early Admissions Document considers the following may be worth remembering:

> they have been constructing and speaking in sentences for only a year or so.
>
> their hand/eye co-ordination and fine motor skills are still developing.
>
> they are physically active.
>
> they are at the intuitive stage of development, finding difficulty in seeing another's point of view or dealing with the abstract.
>
> they can be capable of periods of concentration but may never have had the opportunity to develop this so appear to flit from one activity to another, or cruise around in an apparently aimless way.
>
> they may never have had the opportunity to mix with a large group of children of the same age.
>
> they may never have experienced being left with adults unfamiliar to them.
>
> new situations and experiences can be a stimulus and challenge to some but a threat to others. (23)

The author's own experience has found that when they arrive at school they cannot read and write and during the time spent accomplishing these skills much effort is needed by each individual for relatively modest results in these areas, a phenomenon which is little understood by teachers of older children. A short spell trying to teach middle infants science with what I thought very simple worksheets which required detailed written answers soon showed me the error of my ways!

In addition to this, each child is an individual. Ability to accomplish tasks will vary according to stage and rate of development, home environment and breadth of experience to date. The reception class teacher's task is surely a very difficult one indeed.

So what sort of "work" should these young children be presented with when they arrive at primary school? The answer to this question will depend not only on how we perceive the "nature" of our young children but also upon our understanding of how they learn.

Tina Bruce (24) suggests there are three ways of looking at this.

(a)   The Empiricist View which suggests the child is an empty vessel to be filled.

(b)   The Nativist View which suggests children are pre-programmed to unfold in certain directions.

(c)   The Interactionist View which suggests children are partly empty vessels and partly pre-programmed and that there is an interaction between the two.

In reality the early childhood tradition has not taken the extreme stances of the Empiricist or the Nativist. Recent support for the Interactionist point of view comes from Tom Bower who claims that development occurs as:

> "environmental events interacting with maturationally generated behaviours. The major causal factors in cognitive development are behaviours interacting with other behaviours in their application to environmental events". (25)

This suggests that a child interacts with its environment and within itself. Consequently, adults are not seen as instructors purely giving our information and knowledge but more as the means by which children can develop "their own strategies, initiatives and responses, and construct their own rules which enable their development." (26) Children are supported by adults who help them to make maximum use of the environment. An appropriate environment for four year old children in school can be envisaged by examining suggestions for equipment made in an LEA's Early Admissions Document.

They include:

(1) *Outdoor Play Equipment*
   e.g. slide, climbing frame, carts, trolleys
(2) *Sand Play Equipment*
   e.g. wet sand, dry sand, rakes, spades, sieves, scoops, etc
(3) *Water Play Equipment*
   e.g. water tray, sponge, cork, boats, watering can, etc
(4) *Home Corner Equipment*
   e.g. sink, bed, dolls, table, mirror, telephone, etc
(5) *Imaginative Play Equipment*
   e.g. dressing up clothes, puppets, train set, dolls house etc.
(6) *Book/Library Corner*
   e.g. books, visual aids, photograph albums, magazines, etc.
(7) *Creative Area*
   e.g. paper, paint, pens, crayons, printing/collage materials, scissors, etc
(8) *Table Apparatus*
   e.g. constructional toys, jigsaws, fuzzy felts, dominoes, etc
(9) *Floortoys*
   e.g. large jigsaws, farm, bricks, crane, trucks, etc.
(10) *Science*
   e.g. magnets, magnifying glass, wormery, fish tank, bulbs, etc.
(11) *Musical Instruments*
   e.g. drums, triangles, home made instruments, tape recorder, etc.

Tina Bruce's examination of the work of Froebel, Montessori and Steiner enabled ten common principles of an "early childhood tradition to be drawn up". The author has selected three principles which help us decide on appropriate adult support for children in the early years. The first selection considers planning a theme.

Principle No 3

"Learning is not compartmentalised, for everything links". (27) The aim of nursery and infant school teachers is to provide children with integrated learning experiences rather than to fragment these experiences into subject-based areas. However, flexibly interpreted, subject boundaries can help the teacher to select and plan activities to promote distinctive sets of skills within an appropriate framework.

   D. Fontana states:

   all the experiences encountered by a child have a potential influence upon his long-term development. Thus these experiences cannot be viewed simply as ends in themselves, but should be seen within the context of this development, and should be chosen by the teacher with an eye to those forms of development which society considers to be most worthwhile. (28)

Hence even the teacher of the youngest children in school needs to consider simple study skills, at this stage purely language skills, very simple subject specific skills and key concepts to lay the foundations of Bruner's spiral curriculum. Examples of appropriate experiences could include a museum tabe with old and new objects, regular discussion, handling and change of items. This would be the beginning of historical enquiry. Regular play with different road map scenes or models such as farmyards or villages could promote geographical work. A number of seasonal walks over the course of a year could promote work on nature. Play with water, sand and constructional toys could form the basis of science and technology. Discussion of social issues when and where they arise could be the basis of R E.

   The second selection considers where to start.

Principle No 7

"What children can do (rather than what they cannot do) is the starting point in the child's education." (29) The job most children understand well is how to play. Plato saw play as a means of teaching children the skills of adult work. Comenius recommended education based on learning by doing: "Whatever children delight to play with... provided it be not hurtful, they ought rather to be gratified than restrained from it" (The School of Infancy, 1633). (30)

Children learn about materials by playing with them and continue to learn more at different levels in intellectual growth. A child develops notions of right and wrong behaviour with the help of social play. As a result of these different kinds of learning, the child is constantly forming ideas about the world and about the way in which it works. Through play with materials and people he develops concepts and learns to use thinking skills, the building blocks of the spiral curriculum.

Examples of such learning could include sand and water play in the home corner.

   The third selection considers the type of support the child needs.

Principle No 9

"The people (both adults and children) with whom the child interacts are of central importance." (31) Manning and Sharp suggest that provision of opportunity and materials is not sufficient to provide cognitive learning experiences. They state:

> Without the help of a teacher setting the environment and providing the suggestions, children reach stalemate and their play becomes intellectually aimless... A skilled teacher can point the children's enquiry, provide new materials, stimulate discussion or bring out new possibilities in an existing situation. (32)

The teacher promotes physical, social and emotional development through participation, initiation and intervention in a child's play. Great sensitivity is needed in deciding when to join in and what kind of contribution may be helpful.

A child involved in "Circus" or "Farm" role play for example can be encouraged to talk out what he is doing to help him establish concepts and to acquire vocabulary. This then becomes part of his thought processes, further building blocks in the spiral curriculum!

What content is appropriate to the work of the young child? As mentioned earlier they are at Piaget's intuitive stage of development.

The Science 5 - 13 series suggests that at this stage appropriate objectives are "those concerned with active exploration of the immediate environment". (33) This, and also making use of individual or group interests can help in the selection of appropriate content.

Themes centred on a child's local environment could include "Autumn", "People Who Help Us", "Birds", "Colour", "The Three Little Pigs", "Homes", "Light & Dark", "Gifts", "Babies", "Model Town", "Old People", "The Circus", "The Zoo", "Growing Things", etc. etc.

All of these themes can provide opportunities for visits or visitors and hence development of language work, stimulus for various types of play, ideas for table apparatus and many creative activities.

In conclusion the young child's work should include:

(1) An appropriate learning environment which provides much practical experience.
(2) Cross-curricular learning experiences which have been planned with long term development in mind.
(3) Tasks which begin with what young children can already do well - play!
(4) The intervention of an extremely sensitive adult capable of developing children's play.
(5) Exploration of themes based on the child's immediate environment and interests.

Play and the Subject Disciplines

What is play? The Oxford Dictionary has a large selection of terms which describe play including: "Move about in lively or unrestrained manner... activity... pretend for fun". (34) It can be an extremely emotive word especially when an anxious parent asks his/her young child about what they did at school and receives the answer "Oh we played all day", instead of correctly answering "I engaged in a series of carefully worked out practical activities which lay the foundations of key concepts in the subject disciplines!"

What are subject disciplines? Hirst and Peters (35) broke knowledge down into the following areas: philosophy, moral judgement and awareness, human studies, religious understanding, formal logic and mathematics, physical sciences and aesthetic experiences. In practice, Secondary Schools use the more familiar terms: History, Geography, Religious Education, Mathematics, Science, Art, Music, Physical Education and Craft. The advent of the new G.C.S.E. examination has revolutionised much course work with the emphasis moving away from memorising facts to using characteristic modes of enquiry as suggested by Bruner. The pupils are asked to "act out" the role of the Historian, the Geographer or the Scientist instead of just being passive recipients of numerous facts. In short, they are "playing at or pretending to be the real thing."

What sort of "play" is appropriate to develop these characteristic modes of enquiry? To answer this question we must examine the subject disciplines individually.

History

Joan Blyth in her book "History 5 to 9" (36) suggests History teaching should include the following elements:

Using Evidence
e.g. Pictures, photographs, newspapers, taped interviews, books, museums, old buildings, etc.

Handling Artifacts

e.g. old fashioned household objects reproduction jewellery, costumes or armour, etc.

Use of a Time Line

e.g. placing objects or events in chronological order without worrying about specific dates.

Use of the Narrative

e.g. Rosemary Sutcliffes stories of the Roman Legions. Visiting museums and old buildings.

Using appropriate vocabulary

e.g. Stone age, Medieval, Victorian etc.

Use of Empathy

e.g. using role play to attempt to put oneself into anothers shoes.

Use of these techniques will help to develop the characteristic modes of enquiry of the Historian, skills which can then be used to explore key historical concepts such as:

> Past and Present.
> Continuity and Change
> Sense of Chronology
> Cause and Consequence

Geography

The H.M.I. Curriculum Matters Booklet No 7 "Geography from 5 to 16" (37) suggests the primary curriculum should include:

Investigations of the local environment

e.g. surface features, activities of inhabitants, weather etc.

Study of life and conditions in Britain and abroad

e.g. compare small areas of Britain or abroad with own locality.

Acquaintance with a variety of maps

e.g. O.S. Maps, historical maps, large scale of own neighbourhood, etc.

Techniques of map reading and interpretation

e.g. work on scale, co-ordinates, etc.

Familiarity with globes and with atlas maps.

e.g. identifying continents, oceans, countries, etc.

Of interest is a piece of research by Blades and Spencer which states: "untrained children as young as 3 years old can use maps to locate places in small environments, and that after the age of 4 - 5 years many children can use a map to follow a route". (38)

Use of maps and map skills will help to develop the characteristic modes of enquiry of the Geographer, which in turn can be used to

explore key Geographical concepts such as:

> Similarity and Difference
> Spatial Relationships
> Communication
> Cause and Consequence.

Science

The H.M.I booklet "Primary Education in England" (39) described a curriculum model which split Science into two main areas, Experimental Science and Observational Science. This is a useful way of dividing up such a large area of the curriculum.

Experimental Science.

> "Lancashire looks at Science in the Early Years" states that: "Science is the study of the world about us carried out in a particular way... the scientific method." (40)

This "scientific method" describes the way in which scientific investigations are carried out and includes:

Making observations e.g. a twisted elastic band connected to a propeller makes a model boat move.

Asking questions e.g. how far will the boat move with 25 twists?

Experimenting e.g. carrying out the task and recording the results.

Deducing and coming to conclusions about what has happened based on evidence, e.g. thinking about what actually happened and why. This can lead to the whole process being repeated possibly reaching a general conclusion.

Working in this way teaches the characteristic modes of enquiry of the Experimental Scientist which can be used to explore such key scientific concepts as Energy, Materials and Ourselves.

Observational Science

Observational Science would seem to include those areas of science which are either impossible or unethical to experiment with in the primary school such as animals or the environment. Even though children are unable to experiment in these areas, my experience has shown they do have much intrinsic fascination for children and hence can be used for promoting the skills of careful observation, and identification using simple scientific keys and reference books.

Working in this way promotes the characteristic modes of enquiry of the "Naturalist" which can be used to explore such key concepts as Environment and Alive/Dead.

Religious Education

The teaching of religion in primary schools was originally called Religious Instruction and was concerned with learning the Christian faith in a similar way to contemporary Sunday School. Gradually the name changed to Religious Knowledge (or Scripture), which was content based but looked at other faiths as well as Christianity. More recently the term Religious Education has been used which promotes an awareness of the spiritual side of life within an educational framework. The Schools Council Publication "Discovering and Approach" states:

> religious education should have two sides to it. It is to help children understand the religious traditions of life and thought that they meet in their environment. It is also to help children to be sensitive to the ultimate questions posed by life and to the dimension of mystery nd wonder that underlies all human experience. (41)

The Westhill Project R.E. 5 - 16 by Read, Rudge and Haworth (42) is an example of such an approach. They suggest three sources of content which interact with each other:

(1) Traditional Belief Systems, e.g. exploration of religious beliefs and practices. The project suggests that there is no need to explore all six major traditions in the primary school in equal measure: Christian beliefs and practices could be taught with examples drawn from the other faiths to show comparison. Empathy is an important skill to develop here.

2) Shared Human Experiences; e.g examination of common experiences such as birth, death, joy, sadness, fear, frustration can lead to exploration of "Ultimate Questions" such as "Do people matter more than things? or "What is love?".

(3) Individualised Patterns of Belief in the Classroom: e.g. "But I don't believe in God Miss!" How these emerge or become material for exploration is entirely informal and ad hoc. An objection may arise in discussion or a child may point out a different way of looking at something. The sensitive teacher will always be looking for an opportunity to include and develop these more personal and individual contributions in a way which will benefit the whole class.

Working in this way "touches" on the characteristic modes of enquiry of the Theologian which can be used to explore such key Theological concepts as Self, Religious Traditions, Human Experiences and Choice.

Technology

Technology is a recent addition to the primary curriculum as a seperately identifiable subject. The government definition includes what was known in Secondary Schools as Craft, Design and Technology, Business Studies, Home Economics, Art, and Information Technology. Craft is a combination of Woodwork, Metalwork and work with plastics. Design involves Technical Drawing and a process in which the pupil has to:

> identify the need to be met, assemble any relevant information, and evaluate the effectiveness of the solution. (43)

Technology is the "application of science". (44) Once a problem has been identified and researched a solution is proposed. The pupil is then required to build a "device" or "machine" which will fill the need. Business Studies would involve the pupils in considering commercial applications for their designs. Cookery, Art Work and use of Computers are all tools or skills which could be involved in arriving at "a solution to an identified problem".

The skills involved are:

(1) Identifying a need.
(2) Devising a solution to the need taking into account the reason for the problem to be solved and the availability and cost of appropriate materials.
(3) Making notes and detailed drawings of the solution.
(4) Constructing objects/ sets of objects/ surroundings from the design making good use of appropriate tools and materials.
(5) Improving the performance of the solution and commenting on the final outcome.

Working in this way promotes the characteristic modes of enquiry of the "engineer" and/or "business man" which can be used to explore key scientific concepts such as Energy, Materials and Environment.

How can these modes of enquiry be systematically-organised into a programme of work (or is it play?) for primary aged children? The answer it could be argued is to use a series of Themes or Topics which vary in nature according to the stage of development of the children involved. Piaget's stages of development would suggest that eleven year old children do not learn in the same way as four year old children.

As discussed earlier, the youngest children in primary school learn from interaction with the environment and within themselves. Appropriate Themes are totally cross curricular but subject disciplines should be considered when planning activities which become part of their environment.

The oldest children in the primary school are about to enter the Secondary system and encounter its isolated subject disciplines.

Many years of experience using half termly Themes with a definite bias towards one specific subject discipline has in the author's opinion provided good preparation for the future. Working in this way can avoid common pitfalls of the project approach such as lack of structure; avoidance of unfamiliar areas of the curriculum and contrived work which attempts to bring all areas of the curriculum into one theme. It is also an ideal way of using a theme which will develop a specific mode of enquiry or specific skills which can be used to explore appropriate concepts.

An example of such a theme could be a Geography Project on "The Netherlands". Study skills such as using an index, school library, personal interviews, etc. could be developed based on a geographical content. As well as this, specific geographical skills such as "mapping would be developed. Other curriculum areas <u>are always encountered</u> in each study, for instance, Drama Work, Language Work, Mathematics and Creative Activities could appear in any project but the emphasis would be on developing skills specific to the main theme.

However, a complete programme could not be based on totally cross-curricular themes for Infant children and subject biased themes for Junior children. Again, referring to Piaget's stages of development as outlined in "With Objectives in Mind". (45) Four stages are mentioned, not two! They are:

(1)   Transition from intuition to concrete operations.
(2)   Concrete operations early stage.
(3)   Concrete operations later stage.
(4)   Transition to abstract thinking.

Mentioned earlier was a stage where young children are just beginning to read and write. Joan Blyth, when writing about teaching history to young children states:

> "study of the past can motivate children to want to read, particularly as 7 and 8 year olds outgrow picture reading and one-

sentence explanations of their own pictures". (46)

Mollie Jenkins, a teacher and parent, eventually started her own school because of her dissatisfaction with the type of education schools offered her own children. She writes:

> Now that the children could read, the real fun of learning could begin, although we still spent a brief period each morning on the sheer mechanics of reading and writing (phonetics and work-building, spelling, writing-practice, and so on). For the rest I just let them loose on the largest and most exciting collection of books that I could muster and waited to see what would emerge. All sorts of things did, and developed in the most exciting way". (47)

It could be strongly argued that this is the time to introduce studies where young children are attempting to make a systematic investigation of aspects of the world around them.. Much of the work will be oral, possibly based on local visits to the fire station, the shops, etc. Play activities must be built in to help the children "internalise" new information, but the children will also be motivated to read more and eventually write about their experiences.

Themes with a "<u>slight</u> leaning" towards a subject discipline could provide the framework for such an enquiry. Examples could be The Museum (History), The Fire Station (Geography), Pets (Nature), The Church (R.E.), etc Such themes may be developed in any direction according to the childrens interests, but would still provide a simple framework to include simple subject specific skills.

The three types of theme outlined;

(i)   the totally cross-curricular theme,
(ii)   the theme with a "slight leaning" towards a subject discipline, and
(iii) the theme that has a definite bias towards a discipline

can be used as part of the basis for progression in Thematic work. The next section of the book proposes a curriculum model which will bring together all of the factors which need to be considered when planning progression and balance in thematic work throughout the primary school.

References:

(13)   Place, Time and Society 8 - 13. "Themes in Outline" (1977) Schools Council, P.13.
(14)   Topic Teaching in the Primary School. Gunning, Gunning & Wilson P.33.

(15) Science in the Secondary School Curriculum.

(16) What is Happening in Our Primary Schools - H Pluckrose (1987) P.7.

(17) Teaching Information Skills through Proect Work - D Wray (1987) P.31.

(18) Science in the Secondary School Curriculum.

(19) Topic Teaching in the Primary School. Gunning, Gunning & Wilson P.17.

(20) Ibid, P.20.

(21) Ibid, P.21.

(22) Starting School: An Evaluation of the Experience A.M.M.A. (1986) P.1.

(23) The Early Admission to School of Four Year Old Children L.C.C. (1987) Orange P.1.

(24) Early Childhood Education. Tina Bruce (1987) Hodder & Stoughton P.3.

(25) Ibid, P.6.

(27) Ibid, P.181.

(28) The Education of Young Children. D Fontana (2nd Ed. 1984) Blackwell P.4.

(29) Early Childhood Education. Tina Bruce (1987) Hodder & Stoughton P.181.

(30) Alice Yardley in Fontana. The Ed of Young Children P.265.

(31) Early Childhood Education Tina Bruce (1987) Hodder & Stoughton P.181.

(32) Structuring Play in the Early Years at School.

(33) With Objectives in Mind - Ennever & Harlen (1972) Macdonald Educational for the Schools Council P.60.

(34) The Popular Oxford Dictionary (1980) Oxford University Press.

(35) The Logic of Education. P.H.Hirst & R.S.Peters (1970) Rowtledge & Kegan Paul.

(36) History 5 to 9. Joan Blyth (1988) Hodder & Stoughton.

(37) Geography from 5 to 16 (1986) Curriculum Matters 7 H.M.S.O.

(38) The Periodical "Geography" Blade and Spencer "Map Use by Young Children" (1986).

(39) Primary Education in England, H.M.I. (1978) H.M.S.O.

(40) Lancashire looks at... Science in the Early Years (1986) L.C.C. P.7.

(41) Discovering an Approach (1977). Macmillan Education for Schools Council, P. 11.

(42) The Westhill Project R.E. 5 - 16. G.Read J,Rudge, R. B. Howarth Mary Glasgow Publications Ltd. (1987).

(43) Design and Primary Education (1987) The Design Council, para. 3.4.

(44) The Popular Oxford Dictionary (1980) Oxford University Press.

(45) With Objectives in Mind (1972) Macdonald Ed. for Schools Council P.60.

(46) History 5 to 9. Joan Blyth (1988) Hodder & Stoughton P.29.

A WHOLE SCHOOL APPROACH

Progression

Three specific types of Topic or Theme have been identified as being appropriate to meet the demands made by the changing nature of the Primary School pupil. They are:

Nursery/Reception - The Totally Cross-Curricular Theme

For the very youngest children the bulk of the knowledge/information is new and does not need to be organised into any particular form at this stage other than to ensure that over the course of one academic year a variety of experiences have been sampled which will lay the foundations for later work in Science, Technology, History, Geography and RE. The overriding consideration is that what is presented to be learned is of interest and is capable of catching the imagination of a pupil whose greatest concern is himself. Such Themes/ Topics will be totally cross-curricular in nature and relevant to the pupils involved at that particular point in time.

Infants Year 1/Year 2 - Themes with a slight bias towards the: Sciences (Experimental/Nature/Technology) Humanities (History/Geography/ R.E.)Topical (What is happening now!)

Even at this stage subject boundaries have not yet clearly evolved and the children are still very much concerned about themselves. Themes/ Topics chosen can begin to take on a slight bias towards a particular curriculum area but time still needs to be given over to work that is completely "topical". During the course of one term a "vaguely" Science Theme/Topic may be followed by a "vaguely" Humanities Theme/Topic which in turn may be followed by something purely topical and relevant to the children at that place and point in time. Such a termly pattern could be repeated three times to make up the sructure for one year.

Lower Juniors - The Theme with a Bias Towards a Discipline

Themes/Topics carried out with lower junior aged children can last for approximately half a term and have a distinct bias towards one particular discipline (ie. Science. Nature, Technology, History, Geography or RE.). This would give a curriculum balance over the course of one year and provide many opportunities for first hand memorable experiences and at the very least provide one part of the school year where a particular type of skill (experimenting, mapping etc.) is concentrated on and taught in some depth. In the Topic/ Thematic type of approach it is inevitable that these skills will be used in other themes at other times in the year - they will occur quite naturally - but by earmarking one specific time to teach a certain type of skill in some depth will ensure they are either not missed altogether or merely skirted over several times with little understanding.

Repeating the process over the four junior years provides opportunities to return to specific skills and build upon what has gone before. In the later junior years an even more distinct bias may be given towards the subject disciplines in preparation for the transition to Secondary Schooling.

Balance

Specific subject disciplines have been identified in the National Curriculum as being essential to form a curriculum which is balanced and broadly based. In a Primary School they include English, Mathematics, Science, Technology, History, Geography, Art, Music, PE. as well as RE. A Topic/Thematic approach can be balanced over the course of one year (instead of the more common weekly or even termly balance) by considering the bias towards subject disciplines within the Topics carried out in any one academic year, as shown in the diagram:

NB The diagram considers Science, Technology, History, Geography and RE only.

The National Curriculum During the 1990's

Basic Study and Information Skills will be dictated by the English National Curriculum.

Specific Subject Skills will be dictated by the individual National Curriculum documents in Science, Technology, History and Geography. The S.A.C.R.E.'s will provide information on the specific skills to be developed in RE.

The **Concepts** to be explored will be dictated mainly by the content or subject material to be covered.

The **Content** will be dictated by the Programmes of study found in the individual National Curriculum documents for Science, Technology, History and Geography. The S.A.C.R.E.'s will provide information on the content to be developed in RE.

Appropriate **Activities** and **Experiences** will be provided by the schools and in particular by the individual class teachers in their day to day work of delivering the National Curriculum.

The National Curriculum documents contain **Attainment Targets** which in turn are broken down into **Levels of Attainment** usually on a scale of 1 - 10. If a teacher covers the appropriate content (Programmes of Study) and teaches the relevant skills the outcome will be measured from time to time and recorded for each individual pupil by stating the level of attainment reached in individual Attainment Targets.

In Conclusion

A Whole School Thematic Approach which will deliver the National Curriculum in Science, Technology, History, Geography and R.E.

A whole school approach can be constructed by combining:

(A) The three different types of Topic/Theme which cover the seven primary years.

(B) Themes chosen with a bias towards a number of curriculum areas to provide a balanced curriculum over the course of any one academic year.

(C) Themes that are constructed from Programmes of Study and the Specific Skills identified by the National Curriculum Documents.

BALANCING THEMES/TOPICS OVER THE COURSE OF ONE SCHOOL YEAR

←——————————— **One academic year** ———————————→

RECEPTION

A variety of short (2 or 3 weeks) themes which reflect the interests of the children over one school year may touch on elements of Science, Nature, Technology, History, Geography and R.E.

INFANTS YRS 1 & 2

Vaguely Science	Vaguely Humanities	Completely Topical	Vaguely Humanities	Completely Topical	Vaguely Science	Completely Topical	Vaguely Science	Vaguely Humanities
Vaguely Humanities	Completely Topical	Vaguely Science	Completely Topical	Vaguely Humanities	Vaguely Science	Vaguely Science	Vaguely Humanities	Completely Topical

LOWER JUNIORS YRS 3 & 4

Practical Science Bias	History Bias	Technology Bias	Geography Bias	Natural Science Bias	R.E. Bias
Geography Bias	Practical Science Bias	History Bias	Technology Bias	R.E. Bias	Natural Science Bias

UPPER JUNIORS YRS 5 & 6

Definite Practical Science Bias	Definite History Bias	Definite Technology Bias	Definite Geography Bias	Definite Natural Science Bias	Definite R.E. Bias
Definite History Bias	Definite Technology Bias	Definite R.E. Bias	Definite Practical Science Bias	Definite Geography Bias	Definite Natural Science Bias

←——— **AUTUMN TERM** ———→ ←——— **SPRING TERM** ———→ ←——— **SUMMER TERM** ———→

Infants, Lower Juniors and Upper Juniors could work on a two year rolling cycle for variety.

The rest of this book will be concerned with the practicalities of putting into the classroom a programme of Themes/Topics that will cover the content (Programmes of Study) of the National Curriculum and provide opportunities to teach and use the skills necessary for pupils to work towards the appropriate Attainment Targets.

THE APPROACH IN PRACTICE

Planning a Topic

Some time before a Topic takes place teacher will ....

(1) Decide which area of knowledge she/he wishes to develop ie. History, Geography, Science, Nature, RE., Technology.

(2) Decide on a name of central theme.

(3) Decide on the programme of study she/he wants the children to explore.

(4) Decide on the skills she/he wants the children to develop.

(5) Devise activities that will help the children practise these skills and encounter the programme of study.

(6) Decide on a possible method of organising the children's work.

(7) Decide on the end product required, e.g. a wall display, a class assembly or presentation, class or individual booklets, radio or T.V. programmes etc.

(8) Collect books, posters, film strips, slides, videos, computer programmes etc., suitable for the age group being taught.

(9) Investigate the possibility of a suitable, relevant educational visit or guest speaker.

Carrying Out a Topic

The teacher will ....

(1) Introduce the Topic in as lively or stimulating way as possible to create interest.

(2) Organise the children into working on the various activities, putting right any problems of ability match or lack of resources as they arise.

(3) Help the children discover information, oversee the organisation of group or individual work and to see that each child has a suitable amount of work for its capability.

(4) Encourage individual children to develop ideas of their own connected with the topic

over and above the provision make in school.

(5) Visit the place to be explored and plan a day's activities.

(6) Book a coach, date for the visit, time set etc., collect in money, remind about sandwiches, suitable clothing etc., inform the kitchen that 30? children will be away for the day (most important!)

(7) Devise activities to follow up the visit.

(8) Finish off the work in some way so that the children can see that they have achieved something worthwhile e.g. a 3D model or display; oral presentation; a booklet which they can keep as a reminder afterwards.

(9) Look back at the Topic as a whole and try to assess if she/he has managed to achieve exactly what she/he set out to achieve.

Other Practical Considerations

(A) Organisation of Written Work

When doing projects and subsequently gathering lots of new information it is very useful for the children to compile their own topic "folder" or "booklet". This has several advantages over using an exercise book. e.g.

(1) Children can take great pride if they know that they will keep the finished product.

(2) Making a folder rather than writing in just "another" exercise book makes the topic just a little bit different from ordinary Maths or English work.

(3) A child who has taken great care over a particular topic may request to repeat a sub-standard piece of work and this is more easily carried out with the poor piece of work removed when using a folder.

(4) Similarly, the teacher can request individual pieces of work to be improved.

(5) A folder provides plenty of opportunity for expansion for those pupils who wish to do extra work at home.

(6) A new topic and hence new folder provides a fresh start for those children who felt they didn't do as well as they could have in their previous work.

(7) Duplicated information sheets printed by the teacher on A4 paper can easily be included in the folder.

(8) When the topic is completed it is an easy matter to remove "good" pieces of work for a class display (rather than copying out again). It is important however, to

make sure that the displayed piece of work is returned to the folder when the display is discarded.

(9) Single items of work may be removed to use in group or class discussion providing opportunities for the development of listening and speaking skills.

A good way of collecting well presented and corrected topic work for inclusion in the finished folder is to:

(i) Allow the children if they want to, or are poor writers or spellers, to do a rough copy first. (I often do this with everyone in class when introducing topic work, gradually working towards as many as possible doing a neat copy at the first attempt.)

(ii) After the rough copy has been corrected, allow the children to copy up the work on A4 size duplicating paper. This looks attractive if a 1 cm border is drawn round the outside of the page.

(iii) Finally, draw in any pictures. If each child has a set of lines to rest on the neat copy will have evenly spaced horizontal writing and appropriate spaces may be left in-the text for the inclusion of pictures. e.g.

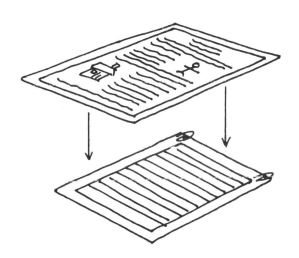

The finished pieces of work are collected together throughout the term of the project in a manilla folder. Finally an appropriate cover is made and all the pages stapled together.

(B) Lack of Expertise!

Some teachers are often afraid to tackle a project in an area where they themselves have not a lot of expertise. Whereas the author agrees that they will probably make a better job in the area they are more familiar with, if for no other reason than they have more confidence in that area, this should not be used as an excuse for not tackling the less familiar. If for example, a Geography student was required to tackle a Science project say on Electricity or a History project on Henry VIII all she/he would have to do is read beforehand an appropriate book e.g. Magnets and Electricity by Ladybird and this would provide 95% of the answers to questions she/he may be asked. The other 5% could be dealt with as problem solving activities and hence would encourage children's research.

(C) Mixed Ability Teaching

The area in which doing a topic scores best over the whole class working from a set book is in the opportunities available for children to work at a level suitable for their own ability. Every teacher knows that a class has bright, average and poor children so the majority of the activities included in one particular topic should cater for at least three different levels of ability. This does not mean that class teaching should not be encouraged. Indeed, it is very valuable at such times as introducing a new topic, getting together to point out a common mistake or as a way of drawing together and finishing off.

(D) Library and Museum Loans

Local authorities generally have provision for schools to borrow a "project loan" from the library service and "artifacts" from a museum loans service. To make good use of these services items often need to be booked some time before they are required.

(E) Two or more age groups in one class

This has for many years been a real problem for schools up and down the country and is now made worse by having to make sure every child receives a National Curriculum.

This is not a problem that an individual class teacher can solve on their own and requires an overall view from subject coordinators/ senior management team/ School Governors / Finance Committee (who directly affect the staffing of the school) and most of all the Headteacher as to how each pupil is to progress from Reception to Year 6.

One solution is for children to progress in "bands" e.g.

The Reception Band.

The size of the reception class/ classes may vary from year to year depending on the intake. This may be dealt with by having a small reception class; a larger reception class with increased support; two small reception classes; a class which increases in size over the course of the year etc. The Reception class would study the types of topics outlined in this book as being appropriate for this age group.

Key Stage 1 Years 1 & 2 Band.

After the reception class of appropriate size to the need, pupils would enter either a pure Year 1 class or a mixed class of Year 1 & 2 pupils. This again may vary in size this being compensated by the level of support given. Pupils should remain in a class of this nature for two years and experience two years worth of "Topics" appropriate to this age group.

Key Stage 2 Years 3 & 4 Band

After two years pupils move up to either single year group classes or mixed age group classes, according to need, where they will be taught for two years. Pupils will study the first two levels of the "Topics" suggested for Key Stage 2.

Key Stage 2 Years 5 & 6 Band

After a further two years, pupils move into the final band of either single year group classes or mixed age group classes where they will be taught for their final two years. Pupils will study the final two levels of the "Topics" suggested for Key Stage 2.

Pupils in very small village schools may need to study the topics suggested over a three (Key Stage 1) or four year cycle (Key Stage 2). Some teachers may choose to split the Science studies into "half-units" so that each area may be studied at two different levels. The author believes it is more appropriate to take time and make the studies practical and relevant for what are still only very young children, rather than to rush and cover the content twice. Good use of the revision unit at the end of the programme will soon refresh young minds. Pupils already have, built into the National Curriculum, the opportunity to visit each concept at four Key Stages (Brunner's spiral curriculum!).

(F)   Grouping of Pupils

There is no ideal way of organising "30" children to work in one room with one adult. I find there is a time for whole class teaching, small group work and individual activity. The following notes taken from "Classroom Organisation for Primary Science" by Simon Naison may give some food for thought,

Single Group For Class Teaching

Advantages

(1)   Maximum interaction with teacher.
(2)   Good input of information and ideas.
(3)   Many teachers find it easiest.

Disadvantages

(1)   Less opportunity for development of skills.
(2)   Difficult to allow for abilities and interests.
(3)   Can make heavy demands on resources.

Individual Enquiry

Advantages

(1)   Development of enquiry skills.
(2)   Children able to pursue own interests.
(3)   Allows children to work at own level.

Disadvantages

(1)   Lack of depth and understanding perhaps.
(2)   Much practical work not viable purely on grounds of the amount of equipment and materials needed.
(3)   Lack of interchange of ideas between children.

Small Groups with Identical Assignments

Advantages

(1)   Easy comparison of measurements and observations.
(2)   Good control of teacher planned activities.
(3)   Easy for recording/assessment purposes.

Disadvantages

(1)   Uneconomical use of resources.
(2)   Narrow range of interest in classroom.
(3)   Space limitations.

Small Group Rotating through a Series of Assignments

Advantages

(1)   All pupils eventually cover same ground.
(2)   Resources can be managed in very systematic way.
(3)   Generally seems to stimulate interest.

Disadvantages

(1)   Little scope for extending children's own ideas.
(2)   Assumes equal time required for all assignments and all groups.
(3)   Places additional loads on the teacher in terms of keeping track of progress in each assignment.
(4)   Cannot sequence experiences for best effect.

Small Groups Pursuing Different but Related Assignments

Advantages

(1) Activities contributing to class interest or topic.
(2) Groups able to pursue aspect of topic to some depth.
(3) Can be economical in resources.

Disadvantages

(1) Less structured and requiring greater teacher confidence.
(2) Greater chance of unproductive effort leading to "blind alley".
(3) The load on the teacher is greater than in the above.
(4) Less able may find it disheartening.

Small Groups with Different Topics

Advantages

(1) Scope for study in depth and experiment design.
(2) Motivation provided by group interests and identity.
(3) Can make good use of resources.

Disadvantages

(1) Lacks dimension of co-operative class achievement.
(2) Harder to maintain progressive structure of content.
(3) The load on the teacher in terms of keeping track of each group and each topic is at a maximum.
(4) Constant cross reporting between groups is needed.
(5) Less able quite unaware of what others are doing.

(G) Organisation of Resources

If a school decides to adopt a Whole School Thematic Approach to the National Curriculum with relatively "fixed" themes or topics then resources can be systematically purchased and stored until they are required e.g:

Posters

A poster bank may be built up using existing resources and planned purchases. A poster pack (e.g. 8/10 posters on a similar theme) would be borrowed by a teacher for the duration of their topic and returned to the central bank after use.

Slides/Videos

Appropriate slides/videos may be recorded or purchased to fit in with chosen themes and kept in a central resource. Care must be taken not to infringe copyright.

School Library

Once a selection of 40 or so different topics have been agreed upon the school library can be checked to ensure it has a range of books to cover each theme.

School Museum

If space allows, artifacts could be donated from the local community to help with History work. I know of one primary school that used the local radio station to help them do this.

Core Book

It is extremely useful when working on a theme, (e.g. Electricity & Magnetism) to have multiple copies of one simple "core" book. Sets of 10 (approx 1 between 3) or 15 (approx 1 between 2) may be purchased and stored centrally.

Technology Resources

A trolley (or two) containing small hand tools and specialized building materials (e.g. balsa wood/corriflute) could be purchased and wheeled into the class working on a "Technology" theme or topic. When this work is finished, the tools and resources would be wheeled to another class working on C.D.T.

Computer Programmes

Word Processing, Data Base, Graphics, Simulations, Control Technology and Concept Keyboard programmes can also be purchased to fit in to particular topics.

Assessment

There has been much debate over the last few years about the practicalities of assessing every primary pupil in every curriculum area on a range of up to six different National Curriculum Levels. As a result the Dearing reforms changed the individual statements of attainment into broad level descriptions and it would appear that through teacher assessment pupils are to be assigned on a regular basis to these level descriptions. A reasonable way forward would be to assess pupils in one curriculum area only at the end of each curriculum unit or "Topic".

SELF EVALUATION SHEET
Victorian Britain Study Unit

Before you start this topic, write down everything you know about life in Victorian Britain:

_____

_____

_____

_____

_____

_____

_____

_____

At the end of the topic, write down, in note form, everything that you now know about life in Victorian Britain.

_____

_____

_____

_____

_____

_____

_____

_____

_____

_____

_____

_____

Compare what you now know with what you knew before you started this topic.

This may be done by using a combination of the following methods:

(1) Making simple notes of skills that are being developed whilst the children are at work can create evidence to support the teacher's assessment of the National Curriculum level individual children are working at.

(2) The use of teacher created or published test papers such as those used for Key Stage 2 Science S.A.T.s can also produce evidence of the National Curriculum level individual pupils are working at.

(3) A simple self evaluation sheet given at the start of the topic and again at the end can give a clear idea of the knowledge retained during the course of the study. The example given is one used for a study of Victorian Britain.

Religious Education in the 1990's: Some Observations

This book has not been written by someone who is an "expert in RE.", but by an experienced Primary Practitioner who has wrestled with the problem of trying to fit a broad and balanced curriculum into a typical school year. During this experience the author has discovered that introducing a Religious Education programme can be a very "thorny" problem because in R.E., more than any other area of the curriculum, we are constantly dealing with sensitive and personal issues upon which parents, teachers, and pupils often hold diverse views.

Why Teach Religious Education?

Three reasons immediately spring to mind;

(i)   Because the Law says we must!

(ii)   Various philosophers believe there is a spiritual side to human perceptions of the world. Consequently to offer an education which does not touch on this area of human thought is to offer an unbalanced view of the world.

(iii)   Our history and culture has been strongly influenced by Christianity. Without an understanding of this, many historical and cultural events are difficult to understand.

What are we trying to do by Teaching Religious Education?

The Really Practical Guide to Primary R.E. by Hubert Smith contains a list of aims for RE., the first of which states one of our aims should be "to provide children with an insight into the nature of religion, and what it means to be religious" (i)

But what do we mean by the nature of religion and what it means to be religious? Let us firstly consider what we should not be doing in Religious Education.

We are not out to convert children to Christianity or any of its particular denominations such as The Roman Catholic Church, The Anglican Church or the Free Churches such as The Methodist Church, The Baptist Church or the United Reform Church.

We are not out to take children on a purely factual "Cook's Tour" of the six major World Religions - Buddhism, Christianity, Hinduism, Islam, Judaism, Sikhism.

We are not out to sell different "Brands" of religion from which pupils are expected one day to make a choice for many people have no faith (Agnostics) and many have reasoned there is no God at all (Atheists). However, the fact remains that there have been many human beings who now, and in past centuries have believed in a Creator or Supreme Power. Various customs and acts of worship have developed from this belief becoming an important part of people's lives. They act in a "religious manner". It is this concept of "being religious" that is to be explored in Religious Education.

This concept of "being religious" can be explored with a group of children by teachers that have a personal faith or by teachers that have none at all through viewing each issue or area of study from the point of view:

"some people believe this - but others do not"

What Elements Need to be Included in a Primary School Religious Education Programme?

Firstly, let us look at the legal position.

Religious Education is to be included alongside the National Curriculum in the basic curriculum which all maintained schools must provide. However, there are no nationally prescribed attainment targets or programmes of study.

Religious Education must be provided for all pupils in State-Maintained Schools including those with Special Educational Needs. This must be non-denominational although teaching about denominational differences is permitted.

Religious Education must be taught in

accordance with the principles and policies determined by the Local Education Authority and set out in an Agreed Syllabus. Modern agreed syllabi are often not prescriptive and consequently open to individual interpretation by schools.

Before the Syllabus can be taught, it must be agreed upon by the local S.A.C.R.E. (Standing Advisory Council on Religious Education) . This is made up of representatives of four groups: The Church of England; other Christian denominations and other faiths which reflect the principal traditions in the area; Teachers' Professional Associations; the L.E.A.

New syllabi (since September 1988) must reflect the fact that the religious traditions in Great Britain are in the main Christian whilst taking account of the teaching and practices of the other principal religions represented in Great Britain.

In voluntary controlled schools R.E. must be taught in accordance with the L.E.A.'s agreed syllabus, although additional denominational teaching may be given at the request of parents.

In voluntary aided schools religious education is in the control of the Foundation Governors who may choose to use the locally agreed syllabus with the addition of appropriate denominational material.

All parents have the right to withdraw their children from R.E. lessons. Similarly, all teachers have the right to refuse to teach R.E. (The author of this book shares the views expressed by Ralph Gower in "Religious Education at the Primary Stage". He suggests that it is difficult to understand why a teacher would withdraw from teaching R.E. when they are not being asked to evangelise for one particular faith but merely teach about religion. (ii)

There must be a daily act of collective worship for all pupils, which in county schools must be non-denominational. Parents have the right to withdraw their children from this.

Daily collective worship may take place at any time during the school day and involve the whole school, parts of the school or other Educational groupings. Schools may not divide the school up into religious groups.

The collective worship in state maintained schools must be wholly or mainly of a broadly Christian character, though not distinctive of any particular Christian denomination.

Schools which have a significant number of children from ethnic minorities may apply to their local S.A.C.R.E. to be treated as a special case.

All of these requirements need to be met in the week by week running of every Primary School!

Current Thinking in Religious Education

Religious Education is a combination of classroom teaching and collective worship, both elements must be present in an R.E. programme.

The Schools Council publication "Discovering an Approach" states:

> "religious education should have two sides to it. It is to help children understand the religious traditions of life and thought that they meet in the environment. It is also to help children to be sensitive to the ultimate questions posed by life and to the dimension of mystery and wonder that underlies all human experience." (iii)

Two distinct types of Religious Education consequently are required.

Explicit Religious Education

This is where a traditional belief system such as Christianity, Judaism, Sikhism etc may be studied. Pupils may be required to learn about places of worship, holy books, leaders of traditions, rituals, festivals, the way of life of a believer etc. The Westhill Project R.E. 5 -16 by Read, Rudge and Haworth suggest there is no need to explore all six major traditions in the primary school in equal measure (iv). Christian beliefs and practices could be taught with examples drawn from the other faiths to show comparison. Ralph Gower suggests that stories which inappropriately emphasise the frightening, cruel and ugly should be avoided and that stories involving miraculous events should not emphasize the supernatural at the expense of the point or the message of the story (v).

Implicit Religious Education

But understanding what it means to be religious requires much more than observing customs and hearing about traditional stories. Smith suggests:

> "If children are to gain all round awareness of what religion entails, opportunities need to be found to 'stir' them, to develop and

encourage a sense of awe and wonder, so that they can learn how to respond to what is beautiful and worthwhile". (vi)

The area of Spirituality is to be explored which includes elements such as prayer, meditation, love, how people feel, why they do the things they do and other tender personal issues. These are very delicate matters which need to be handled with great sensitivity but unless they are touched upon the reasons for people being religious cannot ever be understood.

Jo Moxon in New Methods in Teaching R.E. suggests:

"planning for R.E. should include, wherever possible, examples of explicit religious practice and some deep thinking and questioning". (vii)

In Conclusion:

What Should a Religious Education Programme Include?

The author believes the following three elements must be included.

(a) Specific teaching about traditional religious practices including first hand opportunities to join with the celebration of some common religious festivals.
(b) Sensitive opportunities for children to explore moral issues, questions about self, relationships and the world around us.
(c) Daily acts of collective worship.

Suggestions for an Approach to the Teaching of Religious Education

This book contains suggestions for topics which could be used to teach about traditional religious practices. For Reception classes the suggestions can be found as part of the totally cross-curricular topics outlined. For Key Stage 1 Years 1and 2 the suggestions are to be found in the cross-curricular element of the topics with a humanities bias. At Key Stage 2, topics with a specific R.E. focus are suggested. Opportunities will arise quite naturally within these topics to explore sensitive and personal issues. In addition, opportunities can be created to debate moral issues and explore sensitive and personal issues through the realms of creative writing.(It is envisaged that each child would construct a "Writing Folder" similar to the topic folders mentioned earlier in this book.) The above elements of study combined with the opportunities to take part in different types of collective worship (e.g. Current Affairs, Christian Faith, Other Faiths, Good Works, Class Assemblies etc.) and experience common religious festivals, could provide the basis of an effective approach to teaching Religious Education.

References:

(i) The Really Practical Guide to Primary R.E. - Hubert Smith (1990) -Stanley Thornes and Hulton (p12)
(ii) Religious Education at the Primary Stage - Ralph Gower (1990) - Lion Educational (p120)
(iii) Discovering an Approach (1977) - Macmillan Education for Schools Council (p11)
(iv) The Westhill Project R.E. 5 - 16 HOW DO I TEACH R.E.? -Read, Rudge & Howarth - Stanley Thornes & Hutton (p10)
(v) Religious Education at the Primary Stage - Ralph Gower (1990) Lion Educational (p45)
(vi) The Really Practical Guide to Primary R.E. - Hubert Smith (1990) -Stanley Thornes and Hulton (p26)
(vii) New Methods in Teaching R.E. - Hammond, Hay, Moxon, Netto, Raban, Straugheir, Williams 1990) - Oliver & Boyd (p186)

A SUGGESTED TOPIC PROGRAMME

The rest of this book will offer suggestions for one set of Topics which will cover the National Curriculm programmes of study for Science, Technology, History and Geography. A variety of Religious Education Topics are also suggested. (see diagram opposite)

Some schools may choose to adopt this framework and use it as it stands. Others may choose to select parts of the framework to fit in with existing programmes already in place. Other teachers may choose to use theframework as a reference when planning their own similar topics.

However the book is used, all schools by law now have to deliver the National Curriculum. The author sincerely believes, that even with these requirements, a practically based topic approach should create many opportunities for both children and teachers to have a lot of fun whilst learning in the classroom. Good luck!

A WHOLE SCHOOL TOPIC PROGRAMME

TERM 1	TERM 2	TERM 3

KEY STAGE 1 - RECEPTION - (Topics that are totally cross-curricular)

Autumn	People Who Help Us	Birds	Colour	Winter	The 3 Little Pigs	Homes	Spring	Light & Dark	Gifts	Summer	Teddy Bear's Picnic

KEY STAGE 1 - YEARS 1&2 - (Topics with a slight subject focus)

Science/ Technology Topics	Humanities Topics	Science/ Technology Topics	Humanities Topics	Science/ Technology Topics	Humanities Topics
Ourselves	Around & About Our School	Models from Junk Materials	My First Six Years	Moving Toys	What is an Environment?
Living Things	When Gran & Grandad Were Young	Food Glorious Food	On Holiday	Batteries, Bulbs, Bells & Buzzers	Life in a Castle - (many years ago)

KEY STAGE 2 - YEARS 3,4,5 & 6 - (Topics with a definite subject focus)

Technology Topics	Geography Topics	Experimental Science Topics	History Topics	Natural Science Topics	Religious Education Topics
Design & Make Moving Models (Forces & Motion)	Village, Town or City? (A Settlement Study)	Light & Sound	Invaders & Settlers	In a Wood	Places of Worship
Design & Make Puppets From Textiles (Materials)	Localities in the U.K.	Electricity & Magnetism	Life in Tudor Times	The Body Machine	Special Books
Design & Make Simple Structures (Forces & Motion)	Rhine - River of Europe	Materials & Change	Victorian Britain	In a Pond	Leaders & Teachers
Design & Make Celebration Food (Materials)	World Wide Weather (including a distant locality)	Earth & Space	Ancient Civilisations (Egypt & Greece)	SCIENCE S.A.T. Revision Unit	Living in a Faith

Britain Since 1930 is to be taught as an Oral/Local History Study during English time.

OUTDOOR PLAY EQUIPMENT

Examples could be:
a slide
a climbing frame
ride on toys
trolleys/carts
a swing
trampoline
tunnel
tricycles etc.

SAND PLAY EQUIPMENT

e.g.
wet sand, dry sand
rakes, spades
scoops
sieves
plastic cars and lorries
plastic trains
funnel
moulds
small flowerpots
sand wheel etc.

WATER PLAY

e.g.
water tray
coloured water
sponge
corks
boats
watering can
various containers
various pourers
things that float
things that sink
syringes
droppers
toy pump

BOOK/LIBRARY CORNER

e.g.
books
posters
photograph albums
magazines
cassette player with story tapes
etc.

Computer

With concept keyboard and
appropriate software.

CREATIVE AREA

e.g.
different sizes of paint brushes
paper
paint
clay/play dough
collage materials
scissors
pieces of card
sponges
junk modelling materials
pencils, crayons,
water based felt tips
printing blocks
stencils etc.

NURS
RECE
ENVIR

"An appropriate lea
which provides mu

SCIENCE TABLE

Examples of practical things to try
out could include:
batteries
bulbs
wires
crocodile clips
model lighthouse etc.

NATURE TABLE

Examples of collections
appropriate to the season could
include:
daffodils
bulbs
pussywillow
posters etc.
beans
leaves
seeds eg. acorns/
beech nuts etc
fish tank
with goldfish

MUSIC

e.g.
drums
triangles
tambourines
stringed instruments
tape recorder etc

EQUIPMENT

funnels and tubes
different shaped containers
spoons
whisks
polystyrene tiles
sieve
washing up liquid
bottles
pieces of wood
kitchen spatulas
various funnels etc.

HOME CORNER EQUIPMENT

e.g.
pretend food
table
chairs
sink
dolls bed
table
mirror
fireplace
telephone
writing pads etc.
tea set
pans and cutlery
ironing board and iron, hoover

IMAGINATIVE PLAY EQUIPMENT

e.g.
Dr's set
Duplo/Playmobil eg.
zoo, safari park
farm
dressing up clothes
puppets
train set
dolls house
large jigsaws
bricks
road mat and cars etc.

CRY/ TION NMENT

g environment
actical experience".

TABLE APPARATUS

e.g.
constructural toys such as
Brio or Duplo (Technology)
jigsaws
fuzzy felts
dominos etc.
Plastic Meccano
toys which fix together in
different ways eg. sticklebricks,
magnetic blocks.

WRITING TABLE

e.g.
note pads
coloured paper
shaped paper
various writing materials
including pencils, crayons,
felt tips
stapler
hole puncher etc.

TABLE

Homemade instruments
e.g.
shakers
yoghurt cartons
bottles of water
elastic band pluckers
cardboard box thumpers
sandpaper blocks
hung nail chimers

MUSEUM TABLE

Examples of old objects to
examine and talk about
could include:
old photographs & postcards
old bottles and jars
shoe last
boiler hat
spectacles
camera
clothes
toys
coins
fossils etc.

FAR AWAY TABLE

Examples of artifacts from
distant countries could include:
sweet wrappers
dolls
ornaments
examples of dress
post cards
pictures etc.
holiday brochures
stamps

Alongside "an appropriate learning environment which provides much practical experience" may run a totally cross-curricular theme such as:

Language: Talk about the signs of Autumn. Look at Autumn colour and experience the smells of Autumn. Experience a walk through crisp, crunchy leaves, kick them and see them flood through the air. Make a cool poem or a long list of words all to do with the sights, smells and colours of Autumn. Make an Autumn display including stories and pictures.

Maths: Sort seeds and fruits into sets e.g. hard cases, soft cases etc. Count using leaves of the same kind. Sort leaves according to shape or colour. Count how many leaves are needed for covering large shapes. Fold paper in half and cut out symmetrical leaf shapes.

Science & Technology: Make collections of fruits and seeds and learn their names and match them with the right leaf . Attempt to draw samples. Look at different types of leaves and look at similarities and differences. Learn names of some common trees. Plant bulbs and seeds, water regularly and keep a record of their growth. Choose a tree and look at its structure eg. bark, leaves, shape etc and for minibeasts, nests and birds. Talk about animals which get ready to hibernate.

Humanities: Go for a local walk. Observe Autumnal weather. Look at the shapes of trees, colours of leaves, evidence of fruit. Visit a farm and talk about what happens on a farm during the months of Autumn. On any "expedition" from the classroom talk about directions eg. left, right, forward, backwards also up a hill, under a bridge, past the Church etc.

R.E.: Talk about life-cycles, about how fruits rot down and how seeds germinate into new life in the spring. Talk about harvest time and the gathering of crops for the winter.

Music: Make Autumn sounds with instruments e.g. rushing wind, falling leaves , sweeping up leaves etc. Combine with an Autumn poem.

P.E./Movement/Drama: Dramatise an Autumn poem. Act out parts such as the wind blowing through the trees; the leaves falling in swirling/curling movements, marching through leaves and kicking them.

Art & Craft: Make simple leaf prints. Make pictures from glued leaf shapes. Paint a picture using Autumn colours. Make bark rubbings. Make hedgehogs and other models from conker cases and various seeds. Make seed pictures. Preserve leaves with P.V.A. glue. Make a large Autumn scene/collage.

Alongside "an appropriate learning environment which provides much practical experience" may run a totally cross-curricular theme such as:

Language: Talk about the people who help us at school eg. teacher, secretary, caretaker, nursery nurse, cook, dinner lady etc - how do they help us? Talk about the people who help us at home eg. parents, grandparents, brother, sisters etc and those who help us in the community eg. postman, fireman, doctor, nurse, policeman, dentist etc. Discuss their uniforms, special tools/equipment. Listen to appropriate stories eg. Postman Pat, Fireman Sam, "Topsy & Tim visit the Dentist", Althea books eg "Going to the Doctor", "Going into Hospital", "Visiting the Dentist", "My Babysitter", "Topsy & Tim help the Dustmen".

Maths: Sort into sets different sizes of envelopes. Make a Post Office - sell stamps, weigh parcels. count letters into piles. Make sets of people who do the same job. Make sets of people and some of the tools they use. Make a matching game or a lotto game of people and their tools. Count the number of people who help us each day over a given period of time and make simple charts.

Science and Technology: Experiment with materials: to keep the postman dry in the rain; to keep a policeman warm on duty etc. Talk about the colours of fire engines and police cars. Experiment with colours of uniform which can easily be seen. Look at the lollipop lady's sign, can it be seen in the dark? Make and play with own signs. Make a simple stethescope and listen through it. Make a simple stamper for stamping own letters. Play at doctors and nurses.

Humanities: Observe the people in school who help us; what do their jobs entail? Arrange a visit by a policeman in his car, a fireman with a fire engine, nurse, doctor, road safety officer, postman, dentist etc. Make own jigsaws of all the people who help us.

R.E.: Talk about caring for each other. Talk about people who care for our health, teeth, eyesight and in case of accident. Talk about how I can show that I care and what I can do to help other people. Talk about caring for our pets and birds and animals in general. Talk about famous people in the past who have been caring and helpful.

Music: Learn songs such as the Postman Pat Song and the Fireman Sam song. Compose own simple songs about other people who help us and use well known tunes eg. Here we go round the Mulberry bush, Skip to my leu etc, can have other words adapted to them.

P.E./Movement/Drama: Act out various jobs eg. posting letters, carrying sacks, climbing ladders, fighting fires, directing traffic etc. Choose a job and mime it letting the rest of the group guess what it is.

Art & Display: Collect examples of the tools/equipment/clothing of the different people to make a large display. Look for pictures in magazines and make a scrap book. Make a collage of a road showing all the vehicles which all the different people use. Make a display of toy cars and vehicles. Make individual books on "My Mum" and on each page do a picture of the different ways she helps us. Make junk models of police cars, ambulances etc. Make life size collages of uniformed characters.

Alongside "an appropriate learning environment which provides much practical experience" may run a totally cross-curricular theme such as:

Language: Talk about birds the children have seen and the differences between them. Learn and identify words which represent the parts of a bird eg. beak, wing, feathers, tail etc. Talk about the things birds do during the different seasons eg. Spring - building nests, feeding their young. Summer - having water baths or floating on the waves at the seaside. Autumn - sitting on telegraph wires, flying in flocks across the sky. Winter - feeding from bird tables, swinging on peanut string. Listen to stories about birds eg. "The Owl who was afraid of the Dark", "Spike", "The Little Red Hen", "The Ugly Duckling". Make a display of appropriate books and pictures.

Maths: Sort bird pictures into different sets. Count numbers of birds of the same type. Count the birds visiting the playground and make a chart. Play number games and sing rhymes related to birds eg. 5 little ducks. Make birds nests with shredded wheat and melted chocolate and eggs from fondant icing. String monkey nuts for the birds to eat.

Science and Technology: Talk about size of birds, shape of beaks, shape of feet and their species, functions and properties. Colour simple pictures of birds seen. Make a simple bird table and put out various foods at regular intervals. Observe the birds attracted to feed. Experiment with different types of food. Experiment with things that fly such as seeds and fruits that fall and spin, paper planes, a frisbee, flicked milk bottle tops, paper plates, kites, toy parachutes etc. Observe a pet bird close to. Examine feathers using magnifying glasses. Examine the materials used in a (disused) nest.

Humanities: Stand in the playground and listen to the birds, look where they are. Make a visit to a local park or pond. Make simple maps of the route. Talk about the migration of birds. Display any old nests or feathers. Visit a zoo or wild fowl park. Look at the colours of foreign birds and the noises they make. Look at a simplified map of the world and see where they live.

R.E.: Talk about how we would care for a pet budgie or similar pet. Talk about keeping it warm, feeding it, keeping the cage clean etc. Compare with people. Talk about people in the past who have shown care towards birds and animals.

Music: Listen to tapes of bird songs, also to other sounds they make eg. chirping, squawking, flapping their wings, tapping their beaks on milk bottle tops. Listen to instrumental music which represents bird movements.

P.E./Movement/Drama: Practice soaring, diving, swooping movements, also smaller movements like pecking, hopping, flapping. Piece together sequences of movement. Make actions to the music of "Jonathan Livingstone Seagull".

Art & Display: Make models of birds using yoghurt pot bodies and paper fan wings. Use a variety of materials eg. tissue, crepe, sequins, foil paper, shredded cellophane, feather etc and/or different painting/printing techniques to make birds as masks, mobiles, puppets, collage etc. Make bird silhouettes standing and flying. Make birds nests from plasticine or junk materials.

Alongside "an appropriate learning environment which provides much practical experience" may run a totally cross curricular theme such as:

Language: Make a colour collection and learn to recognise red, blue etc. Have a guessing game - describe a friend/someone in the room with reference to colour eg. colour of eyes, hair, socks, trousers etc. The class guess who it is. Make individual books about colour - find pictures in magazines and stick on appropriate paper with colour words written on. Listen to stories from "1, 2, 3 and Away" reading scheme. Make up class colour poems eg Red is ...., Blue is .... etc. Talk about happy/sad colours, warm/cold colours. Talk about our favourite colours and why we like them. Talk about the colours at home - do the rooms have colour schemes?

Maths: Make sets of coloured objects, enclose in coloured hoops. Colour sequencing using beads, cubes, blocks etc. Make charts of favourite colours, eye colours, shoe colours, hair colours etc. Make pictures involving shape so eg. all squares are red, rectangles - blue, circles - yellow, triangles - green etc.

Science & Technology: Experiment by shining a torch through different coloured filters. Make cellophane viewers. Make a collection of coloured bottles to look through, what colour is the water inside? Blow bubbles and look for the colours. Make coloured spinning tops and observe them spinning. Make pictures using coloured tissue glued onto grease proof paper and mounted on a "sunny" window. Observe drops of oil floating on the surface of water.

Humanities: Look for colours outside. Have a green walk, yellow walk spotting everything you see in a specific colour. Have a walk in the local environment at any time of year and note the colours seen eg. of the trees, flowers, grasses, the sky. Look at colours in puddles. Talk about animal camouflage.

R.E.: Talk about colours found in "our" world. Talk about living in a world without any colour. Try being blindfolded and discuss blindness. Talk about rainbows and listen to the story of Noah's Ark. Listen to the story of Joseph and his coat of many colours.

Music: Sing songs and nursery rhymes which mention colours eg. "Yellow Submarine", "I can sing a Rainbow", "10 green bottles" and songs from "Joseph and his Amazing Technicolour Dreamcoat".

P.E./Movement/Dance: Make movements in P.E. controlled by coloured cards held up e.g. Red = run Blue = walk Yellow = stop etc. Act the stories which mention colours eg "Little Red Riding Hood", "The Little Red Hen".

Art & Craft: Collect shades of a single colour from magazines, birthday cards etc and make a collage. Make a display of one colour a week with objects, pictures, collage etc in that one colour. Mix together 2 colours of paint to make a third. Paint pictures, or use crayons/pastels/felt pens, of rainbows. Paint sunny pictures, night pictures, cold pictures. Use gummed shapes to make brightly coloured pictures. Make butterfly pictures using blobs and folded paper. Use stories like "The Hungry Caterpillar" to make colourful collages.

Alongside "an appropriate learning environment which provides much practical experience" may run a totally cross-curricular theme such as:

Winter

Language: Talk about winter weather - rain, frost, ice, sleet, fog and snow. Collect words to describe cold howling winds; crisp frosty weather - frost on spiders webs, frost patterns on windows; wet muddy weather - splashing through puddles, how does it feel to be wet and cold; feelings of being stuck inside etc. Talk about snowy weather when we want to go outside and play - clean, soft, crisp and crunchy snow, making footprints in the snow, throwing snowballs, building snowmen, sound being muffled. Listen to stories like "Postman Pat goes Sledging", "Postman Pat's Foggy Day", Postman Pat's Letters on Ice", Snowman Postman", "One Snowy Night" by Nick Butterworth.

Maths: Make sets of six snowmen, seven winter trees, 8 Father Christmas's etc. Make a winter counting book. Use peppermint cream mixtures of fondant icing and make peppermint snowballs or snowmen. Count and thread monkey nuts onto a length of strong wool and hang out for the birds. Make bird cakes.

Science & Technology: Fill a jar with snow and watch it melt - what does it turn into? Has it shrunk? Half fill a plastic bottle with water and put into a freezer. How does it change? How long does it take to melt? Do you end up with more or less water than you started with? Make umbrellas using different materials - which is best for keeping people dry? How can we test it? How can we improve it? Make a kite.

Humanities: Go for a winter walk in the school ground/local environment. Talk about directions left and right. Observe how fresh snow makes buildings look different. Why do trees look different in winter? Look for animal footprints. How do people dress to keep warm? What happens to traffic on snowy days? On a windy day - which way is the wind blowing? - look at trees blowing, smoke moving and washing blowing. Listen to stories about Father Christmas. How is Christmas celebrated in other lands, if at all?

R.E: The Christmas Story. Compare with birth stories from other faiths. Consider who needs special care in Wintertime? How do people look after their pets eg. rabbits, guinea pigs etc? What special care do old people need? Who gets them their shopping, tidies gardens etc? Could we befriend some elderly people in the community or visit an old peoples home or write to them?

Music: Listen to music which suggests cold wintery weather. Listen to a sound/video tape of "The Snowman" by Raymond Briggs. Use percussion instruments or invent own instrument to make eg. icy sounds, water plopping, splashing in puddles, rain pouring, wind blowing etc.

P.E./Movement/Drama: Move with the weather's moods: calm slow movements; fast whirling movements; gentle falling snow; fierce biting winds; sharp spiky Jack Frost movements; grow into a snowman etc.

Art & Display: Make a snowy frieze. Make a collage snowman, children sledging, throwing snowballs, snow covered buildings, scarecrow etc. Use block prints to make repeating patterns of falling snow. Cut out snowflakes from folded paper. Make silhouettes of bare trees. Make model snowmen. Make spiky, icy pictures by blowing paint through a straw. Make a montage of magazine pictures to do with winter.

Alongside "an appropriate learning environment which provides much practical experience" may run a totally cross-curricular theme such as:

 # The 3 Little Pigs

Language: Read the story of The 3 Little Pigs. Talk about the story. Decide what might the pigs have taken in their knapsacks? Talk about the houses they each built. How did the pigs feel when the wolf came along? What kind of character did the wolf have? Talk about pigs, what do they eat? How do they really live? Read other stories about pigs eg. "A Pig called Shrimp" - Lisa Taylor. "The Adventures of Sam Pig" - Alison Utley.

Maths: Look at "3". Find examples of things which we find in three - talk about words such as trio, tricycle, triplets etc. Talk about triangles and show the dfferent kinds of triangles, look for triangles. Make sets of threes. Think of stories, nursery rhymes where 3 is mentioned, eg. Goldilocks & The 3 Bears, The 3 Billy Goats Gruff, 3 Blind Mice etc.

Science and Technology: Talk about the materials used for building a house. Talk about the suitability of the materials that the 3 pigs used and why two were unsuccessul. Make models of the three houses.

Humanities: Make a model of the wood where the Three Little Pigs built their houses, showing paths that the pigs walked along, the houses, trees etc. Use materials such as small cardboard boxes, plasticine, playdough, twigs, papier mache etc.

R.E.: Talk about kindness and consideration. Talk about the ways in which we can show kindness to people and animals. Who is kind to me? Look at kindness/unkindness we've shown to others in a single day. Find out about famous people who have shown great kindness to others.

Music: Use percussion instruments to illustrate the story eg. the pigs happily trotting through the woods, the noises of house building, birds singing, shutting the doors the fox stamping through the wood, huffing and puffing etc.

P.E./Movement/Drama: Dramatise the story of the Three Little Pigs. Continue the story - what happens after the wolf has gone away.

Art & Display: Make collages of the three houses. Make large models of the houses using boxes from washing machines etc. Make masks of pigs and the wolf using cardboard plates. Make building tools from junk. Make some playdough/clay food for the pigs to eat. Paint a set of pictures to tell the story like a cartoon strip.

Alongside "an appropriate learning environment which provides much practical experience" may run a totally cross-curricular theme such as:

Language: Talk about types of houses eg. semi-detached, detached, terraced, bungalow etc. Talk about the names of the different rooms eg. kitchen, dining room, sitting rooms, attic etc. What are they all used for? Talk about our own homes - what are they like? If you could choose, what kind of house would you like to live in? Talk about animal homes eg. burrows, nests, caves etc. Listen to stories about homes eg. "Topsy & Tim Move House" by J & G Adamson, "Mouse looks for a House" - Helen Piers, "After the Storm" - Nick Butterworth.

Maths: Look at your own home, how many rooms has it got? How many doors, windows, chimney pots, inside doors, stairs etc. Draw rows of houses and put numbers on the doors. Find a house nearby - look for shapes and patterns eg. windows, brick work, fencing etc. Make a lotto game of animals and their homes.

Science and Technology: Talk about materials houses are made of. Make a display of building materials, talk about why they are suitable. Build houses with different construction materials eg. Lego, Wooden bricks, cardboard boxes etc. Talk about the safety aspect of working on a building site.

Humanities: Go for a local walk. Look for different types and sizes of houses, record the numbers in such a way that they can be recorded/displayed on charts/graphs back in the classroom. Make rubbings of bricks and other building materials. Make a map of the route you took. Look at pictures of houses of long ago and find pictures of houses in other countries where different styles and materials are used.

R.E.: What makes a house a home? In a home you feel warm, dry, well fed and safe - there are people there to look after you. Who lives in your home? Who looked after Jesus when he was young? What sort of a home did he have? Talk about the story of the Wise Man and the Foolish Man.

Music: Make a tape of a selection of sounds that you can hear in your home eg. banging a door, T.V., water from a tap, door bell ringing etc. This Little Puffin - compiled by Elizabeth Matterson - Pub. Puffin Books - a section of this book is devoted to "In the House".

P.E./Movement/Drama: Act out the construction of a house or the story of "The Three Little Pigs". Make bird/animal movements building houses - see "Birds and Animals" in This Little Puffin.

Art & Display: Make junk models of houses, flats, bungalows etc. Small scale models can be made with small cereal boxes. Make a frieze/collage of different animal houses eg. rabbit in burrows, bird in nest etc. Make bird nests from hay and place eggs inside. Print brick patterns to make a wall. Make clay plaques of houses. Look for pictures of different houses in magazines and make a scrap book.

Alongside "an appropriate learning environment which provides much practical experience" may run a totally cross-curricular theme such as:

Language: Talk about buds/blossoms growing on trees, spring flowers eg. snowdrops, daffodils, tulips, new lambs appearing in fields, birds making nests, weather getting warmer, lighter nights and longer days, shoots appearing in the ground, people out with lawnmowers etc - all signs of spring. Talk about animals and their babies and find pictures of them. Listen to stories like "Topsy & Tim Can Garden", "Jasper's Beanstalk" by Nick Butterworth and Mick Inkpen, "The Crawly Crawly Caterpillar" H. E. Todd etc.

Maths: Count daffodils, eggs in a nest, Easter eggs, petals on flowers etc. Make sets of different coloured flowers, large and small Easter eggs, heavy/light, long/short spring buds.

Science and Technology: Grow bulbs indoors and out of doors and keep simple records of progress. Plant enough enabling it to be possible to dig one up every now and then to see its development. Grow cress and other seeds. Talk about what seeds need to make them grow and set up tests to observe this. Collect buds from trees and examine through a magnifier. Take a large bud apart and examine the inside. Make chicks with moving heads or legs using brass paper fasteners or make pop up Easter cards.

Humanities: Go for a walk in the school grounds/locality. Talk about directions eg. left/right, up/down, round/through etc. Look for change - buds on trees, flowers blooming, shoots appearing. Talk about the other changes that have taken place. Observe the clothes that people are wearing. Visit a pond and look for frogspawn. Try and visit a farm or invite animals to visit school eg. lambs, calf, ducklings, chicks.

R.E.: Talk about new life in plants. Hatch some eggs in the classroom and talk about the miracle of life. Invite a mother and baby into school.

Music: This Little Puffin - compiled by Elizabeth Matterson - Pub. Puffin - a section of this book is devoted to "In the Garden". Make up own rhymes/songs about spring.

P.E./Movement/Drama: Act out the growth of a seed from deep in the ground - stretching upwards, reaching the light - opening out into a flower - swaying in the breeze - slowly dying back. Make movments based on "Spring" animals eg. chick hatching out of a shell.

Art & Display: Make collage of blossom on trees etc, sponge paint blossom or chicks. Make chicks or lambs from cotton wool balls. Make 3D daffodils using cut out egg cartons, colour patterns for Easter Eggs, use broken egg shells for Easter Egg collage. Make a farm frieze and name all the signs of springs. Make flowers from tissue paper. Make masks from paper plates of "spring" animals.

Alongside "an appropriate learning environment which provides much practical experience" may run a totally cross-curricular theme such as:

Light and Dark

Language: Talk about the things we do when it is light eg. during the daytime we play, go to school, eat meals etc. Talk about the things we do when it is dark eg. during the night time we stay indoors, go to bed etc. Talk about people who work during the night when we are asleep and the kind of jobs they do. Talk about our feelings when we are in the dark/ in the light. Read stories like "The Owl who was afraid of the Dark" - Jill Tomlinson, "Whatever Next" - Jill Murphy, "Peace at Last" - Jill Murphy, "Burgler Bill" - Janet and Allen Ahlberg", "I want to see the Moon" etc.

Maths: Talk about our day and the hours of light and dark. The things we do each day at the same time eg. start school, playtime, lunchtime, home time, bedtime etc. Use a clock face to show the times. Make a book of pictures to show what you do during the day and during the night.

Science and Technology: Talk about the sun giving light during the day and how the moon and stars appear at night. Talk about nocturnal animals and find pictures of them. Look at pictures of tunnels. Talk about how they are made and what they are used for eg. The Channel Tunnel. Make model tunnels for classroom play, how can we make the tunnel light? Talk about long summer day activities and activities for long dark winter evenings. Talk about shadows and silhouettes - use a slide projector as the light source.

Humanities: Talk about the importance of electricity and what it used to be like in homes before there was electricity. If possible, demonstrate old fashioned lights. Look for examples of different kinds of light. Talk about how the emergency services use lights to warn of danger and the wearing of reflective clothing.

R.E.: Talk about lights used in celebrations eg. birthday cakes, Christmas tree lights, candles in church and in other religious faiths. Look at a stained glass window and talk about the effect that the light has as it shines through.

Music: Talk about and make a tape of Night Sounds and Day Sounds. Make "light sounds" and "dark sounds" using percussion instruments. Listen to classical pieces of music which depict day and night eg. "Morning" Greig.

P.E./Movement/Drama: Mime the sequence of events in a day eg. waking up - getting dressed - eating breakfast etc... going to bed. Mime the movements of the animals of the night.

Art & Display: Make a frieze of day and night showing animals, lights etc. Make silhouette pictures of ourselves or head profiles and make a display. Paint pictures of daytime/ night time; dark colours/light colours etc. In a shoe box/cardboard box make a model of a road/landscape with lid on - night; lid off - day.

Alongside "an appropriate learning environment which provides much practical experience" may run a totally cross-curricular theme such as:

Gifts

Language: Talk about what gifts the children had received at Christmas and on their birthdays. Talk about other occasions when gifts are given eg. birth of a baby, Mothering Sunday, anniversaries etc. Sometimes we may give a gift to someone as a token of our thanks or to show that we are pleased with them. Talk about gifts in the form of talents/ skills eg. being able to sing, swim, play an instrument etc. Talk about famous people who possess certain gifts. Talk about gifts of the earth eg. water, air, fuel, food. Read "Postman Pats Secret", "My Naughty Little Sister and the Fairy Doll".

Maths: Parcel shapes - Cubes, cuboids, cylinder. Esimate the right amount of paper to wrap up a parcel. Wrap some objects up and let the children guess what they are. Put parcels in order of size largest to smallest, heaviest to lightest. Play post offices, weighing, sorting letters, making stamps, paying and giving change.

Science and Technology: Design and make a gift to give to a family member eg. sweets, cakes, a special picture, tube desk tidy etc. Experiment with different ways of wrapping parcels and use a variety of materials eg. brown paper/wrapping paper/tissue paper etc. Sticky tape/string/ribbon etc.

Humanities: Ask the children to bring in gifts they/their parents/grandparents have been given. Put them into sets of new/old/very old. Look at gifts from other countries and using a large atlas find the places of origin.

R.E: Talk further about the earth and its gifts and ways in which we can look after it ie. litter, the countryside code etc. Listen to the Story of the Three Wise Men and the gifts they gave to Jesus. Talk about the importance of giving as well as receiving and the value of the gift. Is the most expensive one necessarily the best? Talk about the importance of saying 'thank you'. Write a thank you letter.

Music: Thinking of a gift as a talent, have a concert where each child can contribute ie. play an instrument, sing a song, say a nursery rhyme, dance etc.

P.E./Movement/Drama: Mime the actions of the postman on his round. Mime the movement of the letters and parcels as they are sorted, rolled, posted etc. Act out the story of someones birthday.

Art & Display: Experience with various printing processes eg. finger prints, potato prints, string printing. Make your own wrapping paper and gift labels. Make a collage of the story of the Three Wise Men. Make a frieze of a birthday party. Use old mail order catalogues to make a collage of gifts for the family - what would you give to each member of the family? Make birthday cakes from playdough. Make parcels for use in play.

Alongside "an appropriate learning environment which provides much practical experience" may run a totally cross-curricular theme such as:

Summer

Language: Look for signs of summer - warmer days, lighter nights, fruits growing on trees, farmers busy mowing the grass or using a combine harvester, blue skies and high white clouds, the smell of summer flowers and fruits eg. strawberries. Collect words to describe summer colours. Contrast with a snowy day, make a class scrap book of words and pictures of summer sounds and smells. Make up holiday postcards to send to each other and post in a class post box. Talk about going on holiday eg. Where we go - how we travel? Talk about summer and winter clothes and why they differ. Listen to stories eg. "Topsy and Tim go on a train". "Postman Pat at the Seaside". "Pat and Jim". "Pat takes off". "Postman Pat's Tractor Express".

Maths: Make sets of appropriate equipment for Winter/Summer/Seaside/Country holidays. Make graphs or pictorial charts of transport used. Make the home corner into a travel agents. Use cardboard boxes to make different forms of transport. Role play buying tickets and giving money. Make a collection of different shells.

Science and Technology: Measure and sketch seeds planted in spring eg. nasturtiums, candy tuft, fried egg plant which will be in flower in the summer. Talk about butter kept in a fridge being hard, but kept outside will be very soft. Talk about foods we enjoy in summer and make a display. Talk about foods which go bad quickly in hot weather. Listen to the story of "The Very Hungry Caterpillar" and other insect stories. Look for minibeasts in the schools grounds. Make model boats and sail them. Make different designs of sandcastles in the sand tray.

Humanities: Talk about summer visits eg. to the zoo, to the park and holiday destinations. Make collections of souvenirs and postcards. Make pictures of how you got there, where you stayed and what you did. Make simple pictures/maps of journeys etc. Try using language spoken in different countries eg. "hello" in French/German/Italian.

R.E.: Talk about being thankful for our world and what we can do to protect our environment; how we can help people in other lands where there is severe shortage of water and famine, the work of aid groups and organisations etc. Collect pictures from magazines and newspapers of people being helped.

Music: Make summer sound tapes of eg. in the park, at the seaside, in the playground etc. Learn summer songs eg. "I do like to be beside the seaside". "I love the Sun". Make summer music with percussion instruments. Listen to classical music depicting the seasons.

P.E./Movement/Drama: Shadow game - copying a partners movements. Traditional games with bats, balls, skipping ropes, quoits etc. Simple traditional English Country Dances. Preparations for Sports Days. Mime different summertime activities and let the rest of the children guess what is happening.

Art & Display: Using the appropriate colours make a long frieze of the 4 seasons. Paint large pebbles from the beach and make into paper weights. Make a fishy scene using a decorated cardboard box with fishes hanging down inside. Make a collage using shells, dried seaweed and sand. Make and paint summer fruits and veg from play dough. Make a large display of tissue paper flowers and colourful butterflies.

Alongside "an appropriate learning environment which provides much practical experience" may run a totally cross-curricular theme such as:

Teddy Bears Picnic

Language: Talk about picnics the children have been on. Where do they like to go for picnics? What do they like to eat? Make simple menus of food suitable for taking a picnic. What other things do you like to do when you go on a picnic? Learn some party games to be used at a Teddy Bears Picnic on the school field or hall etc. and make some party invitations. Listen to stories like "Teddy Bear Baker" - P & S Worthington, the Teddy Bear stories by Gretz and Sage. "Whatever Next" and "Peace at Last" by Jill Murphy, Old Stories by Jane Hissey particularly "Little Bear" also Goldilocks & the Three Bears".

Maths: Make a collection of teddybears and order from largest to smallest, fattest to thinnest, heaviest to lightest etc. Weigh out ingredients for food for picnic eg bread, cakes, biscuits. Count plates, cups, sandwiches etc. Cut into halves and quarters. Make a chart/graph to show favourite picnic foods.

Science and Technology: Design and make place mats and party hats. Talk about containers and the packing of food. Make a basket from a shoe box. Bake bread, cake, biscuits etc. Grow cress, make jelly etc for the picnic. Make teddy bear shaped biscuits and sandwiches. Talk about importance of cleanliness and hygiene when preparing food

Humanities: Make a simple plan of a picnic. Visit local zoo and see real bears. Find out their names and their country of origin. Find out about the country and look for photographs/postcards to make a display etc. Make a collection of very old teddy bears and other old toys. Observe how toys have changed. Make sets of old toys and new toys.

R.E.: Invite members of the community to a Teddy Bears Picnic eg. Senior Citizens or Mother & Toddler Group or Playgroup etc. Ask them to bring along a teddy. Listen to the story of Jesus and feeding of the 5,000 to illustrate the importance of sharing - dramatise the story. Learn or make up own thank you prayer/poem to say at a picnic.

Music: Learn traditional out of door action songs eg. "The Farmer's in his Den", "The Big Ship sails through the Ally-Ally-o; also skipping songs and catching songs. Sing "Teddy Bears Picnic".

P.E./Movement/Drama: Move like a teddy bear. Move like a puppet and other toys you might find in a toy shop. Make up a drama to the music of "Teddy Bears Picnic".

Art & Display: Paint or print a picture of your teddy bear. Make a teddy with moving arms and legs. Make a frieze/collage picture of teddy bears picnic. Make plates of play dough food for a pretend picnic. Make paper flower table decorations. Cut out pictures of food from magazines and stick on to paper card plates. Make teddy bear masks from paper plates or half masks which do not cover the mouth and nose.

PROGRAMME OF STUDY

Pupils should be taught:
- that humans move, feed, grow, use their senses and reproduce
- to name the main external parts, e.g. *hand, elbow, knee,* of the human body
- that humans need food and water to stay alive that taking exercise and eating the right types and amount of food help humans to keep healthy
- about the role of drugs as medicines
- that humans can produce babies and these babies grow into children and then into adults
- that humans have senses which enable them to be aware of the world around them
- to recognise similarities and differences between themselves and other pupils
- to design and make their own products
- to take apart simple manufactured products to learn how they function; assess the quality of a product; consider safety at all times and use appropriate vocabulary for equipment, materials and components used.

SKILLS TO BE DEVELOPED

- to turn ideas suggested to them, and their own ideas, into a form that can be investigated
- to think about what is expected to happen when planning what to do
- to recognise when a test or comparison is unfair
- to explore using appropriate senses
- to make and record observations and measurements
- to communicate what happened during their work
- to use drawings, tables and bar charts to present results
- to make simple comparisons
- to use results to draw conclusions
- to indicate whether the evidence collected supports any prediction made
- to try to explain what they found out

When Designing - generate, discuss and develop ideas; communicate designs through sketches and models; improve original ideas and decide how to proceed.

When Making - select tools; measure, mark out, cut and shape materials; assemble, join and combine materials and   components; finish off and evaluate the product.

SUPPORTING CURRICULUM LINKS

English	-	Write: My earliest memories; What I do in my spare time; When I grow up; My favourite things are; descriptions of experiments etc.
Maths	-	Bar charts for hair/eye colour, height, age etc. Shape - 2D circles, squares, triangles, rectangles, 3D cylinders, spheres, cubes, cuboids etc. Sorting - size, shape, colour etc.
History	-	Make a time chart showing how my body has developed over the last 5 years.
Geography	-	Examine large scale maps to examine where we live.
P.E.	-	Devise and carry out a simple keep fit routine on a regular basis. Explore different types of movement.
R.E.	-	Talk about how we like to be treated by others.

TALK ABOUT

- features of the face e.g. shapes, colours, size.
- position of the different features.
- how features change to show different emotions.
- similarities and differences of faces in the class.
- the five senses.
- our "fuel" to make us move.
- good health, food and exercise.
- safety in the home.
- how we look after babies.
- looking after younger brothers and sisters.
- how people grow and the stages they go through.
- what happens to us when we are ill.
- where medicines should be kept.
- the importance of keeping clean.

ACTIVITIES

Sort junk materials into 'shape' collections for later use.

Experiment with paints, glues, materials e.g. mixing paints for skin materials, glueing materials onto card etc.

Make a 3D face from junk materials based on a paper plate. Apply appropriate finishings.

Make a moving body. Cut out printed sheets/provide pre-cut parts according to ability. Make holes (e.g. punch, bradawl, pointed lolly sticks) and colour figures appropriately. Join the figures in the correct order with paper fasteners.

Experiment with the five senses e.g.:
Devise and carry out simple eye tests.
Listen through ear trumpets and string telephones.
Blindfold pupils and ask them to identify various tastes.
Blindfold pupils and ask them to identify various smells.
Identify objects by feeling them in a bag.

STARTING POINTS

Looking at the children's faces; self portraits - they must have a mirror to look into :- looking at each other.

Naming the parts of the body, tie in with nursery rhymes and songs e.g. 'Heads and Shoulders, Knees and Toes', 1 Finger 1 Thumb Keep Moving' etc.

Make a collection of a wide range of reclaimed materials for pupils to freely experiment with i.e. cutting, tearing, joining.

Make, draw or study a full size skeleton.

Interview a parent about his/her new baby.

Useful Books
Topsy and Tim go to the Doctor/Dentist etc. - Pub. Blackie.
Littlebody Books - Eyes, Teeth, Hands etc. - Pub. Macdonald.
How Your Body Works - Pub. Usborne.
How to make Pop-Ups - Pub. Usborne.

RESOURCES/EQUIPMENT

Wide choice of reclaimed materials, scissors, safety snips, glues (pva, wallpaper paste, glue sticks etc.), sticky tape (sellotape, double-sided, brown gummed tape etc.).

Paints for finishing (showing children pva mixed with paint covers junk materials well, sandpapering yoghurt pots ensures paint with pva covers and adheres to plastic).

Possible Visits
Local clinic, doctors surgery, health centre, hospital, dentist, opticians.

Possible Visitors
School nurse, mother and baby i.e. physical change/ growth, school dentist.

Best Time of Year
Any.

Ourselves

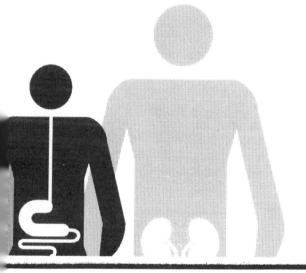

ART AND DISPLAY

Display a range of portraits by different artists working in different styles. Include a mirror and dressing up clothes as part of the display.

Talk about portraits from the past and how they differ from now.

Paint/draw portraits of each other/one child in the style of or colours chosen by a particular artist.

Paint/draw self portraits using a mirror.

Make silhouettes of children produced using an overhead projector - identify who is who.

Collect and display colours, patterns, pictures, objects in a box about me.

Make finger prints; enlarge and develop into a pattern.

Print patterns using hands; look at Richard Long's hand circle designs.

Make a model of yourself out of clay/plasticine.

Make a tile face.

DIRECTED PLAY

Sand and Water
Senses - touch - feeling the sand with hands and feet.
Changing the sand condition from dry to wet.
Changing the water colour - senses - sight.

Role Play
Turn role play area into hospital, dentist, surgery, clinic etc. Make up little plays using puppets and the jointed figures.

Imaginative Play
Match faces to connect body (game). Play with Barbie/ Sindy type figures in dolls house; cars on road mat making the school run etc.

Play with Constructional Toys
Stickle Bricks - making people.
Teacher make jointed figures for disassembling.
Tasks involving paper fasteners, nuts and bolts.

END PRODUCT

Display of pupils 3D faces made from junk materials; can the pupils recognise their friends?

Simple descriptions of eye/hair colour, skin colour etc.

Simple plays made up using the jointed figures performed to an audience of reception children/ parents/whole school etc.

If time, let the children create their own jointed figure of a person (real or imagined) or of an animal.

Make a "Myself Book".

Use the data base program to answer various questions about the class as a whole.

Devise a "sound" or "smell" or "memory" quiz to try out on others.

Prepare a class assembly to tell the whole school how to look after our bodies.

Write a class poem telling "what is unique about our class".

PROGRAMME OF STUDY

Pupils should study the locality of the school. The locality of the school is its immediate vicinity; it includes the school buildings and grounds and the surrounding area within easy access.

Pupils should be taught:
- about the main physical and human features, e.g. *rivers, hill, factories, shops*, that give the localities their character.
- how localities may be similar and how they may differ, e.g. *both areas may have farmland, but animals may be kept on the farms in one area, while in the other crops may be grown*
- about the effects of weather on people and their surroundings, e.g. *the effect of seasonal variations in temperature on the clothes people wear*
- how land and buildings, e.g. *farms, parks, factories, houses*, are used.

SKILLS TO BE DEVELOPED

- observe, question and record, and to communicate ideas and information
- use geographical terms, e.g. *hill, river, road*, in exploring their surroundings
- undertake fieldwork activities in the locality of the school, e.g. *observing housing types, mapping the school playground*
- follow directions, including the terms up, down, on, under, behind, in front of, near, far, left, right, north, south, east, west
- make maps and plans of real and imaginary places, using pictures and symbols, e.g. *a pictorial map of a place featured in a story, a plan of their route from home to school*
- use globes, maps and plans at a variety of scales; the work should include identifying major geographical features, e.g. *seas, rivers, cities*, locating and naming on a map the constituent countries of the United Kingdom, marking on a map approximately where they live, and following a route
- use secondary sources, e.g. *pictures, photographs (including aerial photographs), books, videos*, CD-ROM encyclopaedia, to obtain geographical information.

SUPPORTING CURRICULUM LINKS

English - Children write letters to the local council about what they like and dislike about the local area and what they would like to change.

Maths - Measurement exercises around the school building.

Technology - As a class produce a 3D model of the school from junk materials.

I.T. - Direct a roamer around a large scale map of the school.

History - Look for evidence of the past in the buildings around the school. Talk to people who have lived locally for many years.

R.E. Element Make several visits to examine the inside and outside of some local places of worship. Talk about what a church looks like; are all churches the same?; who has been to a Sunday Service/Christening/a Church Wedding; what happens at such events; what is a hymn?; what does it mean to pray?; what sort of people go to church?; who is in charge?; what may be found in the church grounds?; etc. Reflect on the reasons for such buildings existing.

TALK ABOUT

- Their address in the form of street, town and country.

- How the land and buildings, they have seen on their 'Walkabouts' are used.

- The jobs carried out in the local community and school.

- How people entertain themselves. What can they do? Where can they go?

- Their likes and dislikes in the local area and changes they would like to see.

- What they can see in photographs of their local area.

- What they interpret on large scale maps of the area.

- Landmarks they pass on their way to school.

ACTIVITIES

Make a large map of the school and neighbouring streets and trace the children's walkabout.

Follow a set of directions to lead you to a hidden "treasure" in the school grounds.

Discuss and develop symbols for local features i.e. river, factories, shops, church and place these on the map. Children work in groups. Can they place the symbols in the correct location?

Children draw the route from their home to school. Draw on any features they pass.

Look at local maps and aerial photographs which include the school. What can the children recognise? Discuss.

Children bring in a photo of their house. Locate where the children live on the map. Match photo to location with a string.

Take photographs of features in local area. Children sort into categories: where we worship, relax, where people live, shop, work etc.

List jobs and roles in the local community. What would they like to be?

STARTING POINTS

A Brainstorm - what do the children already know about their own immediate locality, likes/dislikes?

"Walkabout" the surrounding area. Follow their route on simple maps (drawn by the teacher). Make notes of the main physical and human features observed.

Useful Books

Information Books-
Look around the school, street, park, shops (Look around series Wayland) - Clive Pace, Jean Birch.
All about your street - Stephen Scoffham.
Safe and Sound - Around the Town - Out and About - L Baillie, P Shuckburgh.

Story Books-
On my way to school - Celia Berridge.
Stories from our street - R Tulloch, J Vivas.

RESOURCES/EQUIPMENT

Local reference books.
Aerial photographs, maps and plans.
Pictures/photographs of local area.
Reference books/information books about houses, shops, streets etc.

Possible Visits
Local place of worship.
One particular street which can be studied.
A "Walkabout" the local area. Visit a local factory, shop, bakery etc.

Possible Visitors
People who work in the local community i.e. police officer, local shopkeeper etc.

Best Time of Year
Spring or summer. Good weather is required for walkabouts!

Around & About Our School

ART AND DISPLAY

Make a display of photographs of unusual/unexpected parts of the school e.g. boiler house, kitchen pantry etc. Can the children identify them?

Look for shapes around the school e.g. doors/windows. Look for patterns to recreate e.g. bricks, railings, tiles etc. Look for colours; patterns in stonework, curtains etc. to collect, draw and enlarge.

Design a new sign for the school.

Make a class collage or painting of the school.

Scale up one child's drawing of school using O.H.P. and all children draw or paint themselves to go around it.
Make junk models of shops or houses near school.
Design or model a new school playground.
Design and draw signs which show people how to find their way around the school.

DIRECTED PLAY

Sand and Water
Make the sand tray into a builder's site. Experience the texture of wooden bricks, house bricks, sand and other building materials. Build a bridge strong enough to span the water by experimenting with the water tray.

Role Play
Following a visit to a local place of work i.e. shop, bakery, factory; create an area based on this business.

Imaginative Play
Use 3D model of school and surrounding area. Use toy cars, lego people etc. to act out situations, daily life. Alternatively play with road floor maps.

Play with Constructional Toys
Design a new play area for the school playground.

END PRODUCT

Display board containing large map of school and surrounding area including features, road names, where the children live etc.

A booklet containing the children's local information sheets which can be shown to visitors to the school from outside the local area, or a copy of which can be sent to a Link school.

A class newspaper - reports written by the children and pictures of local incidents during the time of the topic.

A class assembly all about their locality. Invite local 'celebrities' i.e. the local bobby, lollypop lady etc.

Children's individual topic work displayed in individual topic folders.

PROGRAMME OF STUDY

Pupils should be taught:
- to use their senses to explore and recognise the similarities and differences between materials
- to sort materials into groups on the basis of simple properties, including texture, appearance, transparency and whether they are magnetic or non-magnetic
- to recognise and name common types of material, e.g. *metal, plastic, wood, paper, rock*, and to know that some of these materials are found naturally
- that many materials, e.g. *glass, wood, wool*, have a variety of uses
- that materials are chosen for specific uses, e.g. *glass for windows, wool for clothing*, on the basis of their properties
- to design and make their own products
- how to make their structures more stable and withstand greater loads
- to take apart simple manufactured products to learn how they function; assess the quality of a product; consider safety at all times and use appropriate vocabulary for equipment, materials and components used.

SKILLS TO BE DEVELOPED

- to turn ideas suggested to them, and their own ideas, into a form that can be investigated
- to think about what is expected to happen when planning what to do
- to recognise when a test or comparison is unfair
- to explore using appropriate senses
- to make and record observations and measurements
- to communicate what happened during their work
- to use drawings, tables and bar charts to present results
- to make simple comparisons
- to use results to draw conclusions
- to indicate whether the evidence collected supports any prediction made
- to try to explain what they found out

When Designing - generate, discuss and develop ideas; communicate designs through sketches and models; improve original ideas and decide how to proceed.

When Making - select tools; measure, mark out, cut and shape materials; assemble, join and combine materials and components; finish off and evaluate the product.

SUPPORTING CURRICULUM LINKS

English	-	Make word banks to describe building materials. Write a description or a story about someone who lives in your building.
Maths	-	3D shape. Sorting of materials.
Science	-	Use magnets to search for magnetic materials.
History	-	Look for evidence of old fashioned/modern buildings. Look for evidence of ageing.
Geography	-	Make maps of walk around locality. Make plans of model houses or one room in the house.
Music	-	Learn songs about buildings e.g. "The wise man built his house upon the rock".
R.E.	-	Look at pictures of churches. Talk about how they are different from other buildings.

TALK ABOUT

- Types of houses/buildings found close to school.
- Materials used to make buildings.
- Which materials are similar/different.
- Which materials are natural/man-made.
- Which materials are magnetic/non magnetic.
- The names of common building materials.
- The uses of specific materials.
- What uses are made of different buildings.
- How to build a stone/brick wall.
- What rooms are found in different buildings.
- The task of constructing a model building.
- The range of junk materials available.
- How the materials can be cut, glued, painted, covered, joined, folded, hinged etc.
- How to stay safe when working with tools.

ACTIVITIES

Make model buildings working in a group.

Divide large boxes into rooms for the model building.

Construct a roof by scoring and bending.

Choose and mark positions for doors and windows. (Health and Safety: Adult to cut out with craft knife).

Select wallpaper for interior walls and stick with appropriate glues.

Select materials for floor coverings and fix.

Examine examples of model furniture. Select appropriate sized junk materials and construct items of furniture. Discuss colour coordination and look at design books on interiors.

When inside complete, finish outside appropriately.

At all times, experiment with the best tools to do each job and the most appropriate glue for each joining.

STARTING POINTS

Walk around the local area. Take photographs and make wall rubbings.

Make sketches and talk about buildings observed.

Collect different building materials for sorting.

Divide pupils into groups for creating a chosen building seen near to the school.

Give each group a large box and inform them they are to make them into the given building.

Discuss what is found inside buildings. Examine appropriate catalogues and books.

Useful Books
First Learning - Shape - Usborne Books.
Design and Decorate Your Room - Usborne Books.
How to Draw Buildings - Usborne Books.
How Things are Built - Usborne Books.
Picture Wordbook - The House - Usborne Books.

RESOURCES/EQUIPMENT

Junk materials, appropriate tools, glues, tapes, a selection of wallpapers (old wallpaper books), selection of fabrics etc.
One large box per group.
A range of carpet cut offs.
Building materials e.g. bricks, stone, tiles, glass, wood, sand, cement etc.

Possible Visits
Walking around the local environment.
Building site.
Local museum.
Estate Agents.

Possible Visitors
Bricklayer, architect, stainglass window maker to talk about their work.

Best Time of Year
Any - although fine weather is needed for walks and sketching.

Models from Junk Materials

ART AND DISPLAY

Display a range of junk materials. Label naming shapes and materials manufactured from.

Talk about how the junk can be changed. Groups work on one type e.g. egg boxes and demonstrate all the things they can do to them e.g. experiment with different types of paints for finishing off, different ways of glueing, different coverings which can be stuck on etc.

Make observational drawings of models made from junk materials.

Design a house, a vehicle, a person, an animal that could be made from junk. Write a story about it.

Look at examples of sculpture using different materials e.g. stone, metal, Picasso's bull head from handlebars etc.

DIRECTED PLAY

Sand and Water
Making sandcastles - dry and wet sand. The tallest tower possible in wet sand. Make from different shaped containers available. Floating/sinking experiments with building materials.

Role Play
House corner could be changed into a variety of rooms. Let the pupils design and print wallpaper and paper a wall in the house corner.

Imaginative Play
Pupils imagine being local estate agents. Make For-Sale signs for model farm/castle. Write sales details and name a price. Hold a farm auction.

Play with Constructional Toys
Building blocks, Lasy, Duplo, Lego. Experiment with different blocks used for walls. Find the strongest pattern of bricks to be used.

END PRODUCT

Display model buildings constructed.

Sketch/paint pictures of finished houses and display alongside a picture of the actual house or initial designs.

Plans drawn of the buildings constructed.

An accurate written description of model.

Structured play with toy figures in the houses constructed.

A model street complete with name and numbered houses.

Model people created to live in the street, work in the shops etc.

Stories about the people who live in/use the buildings.

PROGRAMME OF STUDY

Pupils should be taught:
- to investigate changes in their own lives
- about the everyday life, work, leisure and culture of men, women and children in the past, e.g. clothes, diet, everyday objects, houses, shops and other buildings, jobs, transport entertainment.

At "Story" and "Assembly" times:
Pupils should be taught about the lives of different kinds of famous men and women, including personalities drawn from British history, e.g. rulers, saints, artists, engineers, explorers, inventors, pioneers.
Pupils should be taught about past events of different types, including events from the history of Britain, e.g. notable local and national events, events in other countries, events that have been remembered and commemorated by succeeding generations, such as centenaries, religious festivals, anniversaries, the Gunpowder Plot, the Olympic Games.

SKILLS TO BE DEVELOPED

- to be able to sequence events and objects, in order to develop a sense of chronology
- to be able to use common words and phrases relating to the passing of time e.g. old, new, before, after, long ago, days of the week, months and years
- to be able to investigate aspects of the past through stories from different periods and cultures, including stories and eyewitnesses accounts of historical events
- to be able to recognise why people did things, why events happened and what happened as a result
- to be able to identify differences between ways of life at different times
- to be able to identify different ways in which the past is represented e.g. pictures, written accounts, films, plays, songs, replica objects and museum displays
- to be able to find out about aspects of the past from a range of sources of information, including artefacts, pictures and photographs, adults talking about their own past, written sources, and buildings and sites
- to ask and answer questions about the past.

SUPPORTING CURRICULUM LINKS

English   -   Record incidents and anecdotes from the children's babyhood in a class book. Use common words and phrases relating to passage of time.

Maths   -   Discuss changes in size. Talk about taller than/shorter than. Compare birth weights.

Geography   -   Locate birthplaces on maps.

I.T.   -   Record own strongest memory on wordprocessor. Make into a class book of memories.

Music   -   Listen to lullabies. In groups compose a short piece of quiet, soothing, gentle sounds to make a baby fall asleep.

R.E. Element: Hold a mock Christening. Choose roles for different members to play. Choose an appropriate name for the doll or dolls to be Christened. Ask a Clergyman to 'Christen' your doll. Hold a family celebration afterwards. Interview the Clergyman to find out how he/she hears of new babies to be named and the preparations that need to be made. Listen to accounts of how a baby is named in religious traditions other than Christianity. Make copies of Baptismal Certificates.

TALK ABOUT

- How the children are aware of their own growth and change i.e. clothes and shoes become too small.

- The things they can do now which they couldn't do a year ago, two years ago etc.

- The things a younger brother/sister cannot do.

- How they behaved as babies, what they ate, wore, did, where they slept and sat and what they played with.

- Incidents and recount anecdotes from their own babyhood and early childhood.

- How a family prepares for a new baby.

- How we are all different and grow/develop at different rates.

ACTIVITIES

Children bring in evidence of their own "birth" day i.e. birth certificates, tags, cards, newspaper reports, birthday book, 1st photograph etc. Such artefacts can be discussed, information discovered and compared and displayed.

Collect photos of them as babies, toddlers and as they are today. Sequence photographs in a time line and compare.

Draw their own time lines showing how they have grown bigger and stronger through the years; how they have worn different clothes; have eaten different food and played with other kinds of toys.

Collect in toys and sort into appropriate age groups. Shoes or clothes can also be sequenced.

Invite parents to bring younger children or babies to visit the class. Question what can't the babies do that the children now can.

Make a 'Birthday Train' with a carriage for each month. The children draw themselves and put their drawing in the correct carriage on their birthday.

STARTING POINTS

Make collections of toys and clothes which can then be sorted into appropriate age groups.

Tell the children about your own childhood. Show photographs and share memories.

Bring in "birth" memorabilia and encourage the children to do the same.

Useful Books
Ben's Baby - Michael Foreman.
Welcome Little Baby Aliki - Bodley Head.
Happy Birthday Sam - Pat Hutchins.
You'll Soon Grow into them Titch - Pat Hutchins.
How you Grow and Change - Dorothy Baldwin/Claire Lister.

RESOURCES/EQUIPMENT

Reference books on the themes of babyhood, early childhood, growing up etc.

Pictures/posters showing children at different ages and stages of development.

Photographs, artefacts, clothes, toys etc. of children at different ages.

Possible Visits
To a baby clinic.
To the local nursery or playgroup to see how children are developing.

Possible Visitors
A Health Visitor.
Parents with younger children or babies.
Midwife.

Best Time of Year
Autumn term, although any time will do.

My First Six Years

ART AND DISPLAY

Put on display pictures of children as babies - and now as six years old - list what has changed.

Draw, paint a series of pictures of e.g. 3 things that have happened to me since I was born (that are of importance or that I remember well).

Draw, paint:

clothes then	-	clothes now
food then	-	food now
toys then	-	toys now
friends then	-	friends now
pastimes then	-	pastimes now
books then	-	books now

Actual items, objects could also become part of a display.

Draw your room how you would like it now - how it would be for a baby.

Draw round a baby, hand or foot - put a drawing of your own next to it.

Make a picture/book alphabet frieze for a baby - Design a wallpaper or write a story (comic book style) for a six year old.

DIRECTED PLAY

Sand and Water
Explore bathtime. Children bring in toys that they play with in the bath now and compare with toys they used when younger. Items can include sponges, old shampoo bottles, clockwork bath toys etc. Develop children's awareness of capacity/volume.

Role Play
A Health Centre or Baby Clinic - waiting room/ medical room, doctors, nurses, patients, receptionist etc.

Imaginative Play
In small groups with adult supervision/intervention if necessary produce a short play about the addition of a new baby to a family.

Play with Constructional Toys
Design and make a moving toy for a toddler. Discuss why small objects would not be suitable (safety).

END PRODUCT

Class book of memories, anecdotes and incidents, including best written work, word processing, pictures put on display in book corner.

Display of birthday artefacts and time lines of photographs, clothes and toys.

Children make their own zig-zag book made up of photographs of them placed in the correct chronological order.

Large-scale class time line on display showing date started school and added to during the year with 'Our Assembly', 'Our Christmas Play' etc. This can be done by pegging events onto a washing line in order. At the end of the year look back and discuss events.

PROGRAMME OF STUDY

Pupils should be taught:
- to describe the movement of familiar things, e.g. *cars getting faster, slowing down, changing direction*
- that both pushes and pulls are examples of forces
- that forces can make things speed up, slow down or change direction
- that forces can change the shapes of objects
- to design and make their own products
- to use simple mechanisms, including wheels and axles, and joints that allow movement
- to take apart simple manufactured products to learn how they function; assess the quality of a product; consider safety at all times and use appropriate vocabulary for equipment, materials and components used.

SKILLS TO BE DEVELOPED

- to turn ideas suggested to them, and their own ideas, into a form that can be investigated
- to think about what is expected to happen when planning what to do
- to recognise when a test or comparison is unfair
- to explore using appropriate senses
- to make and record observations and measurements
- to communicate what happened during their work
- to use drawings, tables and bar charts to present results
- to make simple comparisons
- to use results to draw conclusions
- to indicate whether the evidence collected supports any prediction made
- to try to explain what they found out

When Designing - generate, discuss and develop ideas; communicate designs through sketches and models; improve original ideas and decide how to proceed.

When Making - select tools; measure, mark out, cut and shape materials; assemble, join and combine materials and components; finish off and evaluate the product.

SUPPORTING CURRICULUM LINKS

English	-	Match words to appropriate pictures e.g. parts of a bicycle, car, boat, plane etc. Write about blowing bubbles.
Maths	-	Directions - left, right, forwards, backwards etc. Measure how far various wheeled toys travel down a slope.
History	-	Visit a museum of childhood. Make a collection/examine old fashioned toys.
Geography	-	Examine toys for places of manufacture. Locate on globe or world maps.
P.E.	-	Explore pushing and pulling movements. Experiment with moving various sizes of balls. Invent new ball games. Play games which involve getting faster, slowing down and changing direction. Think about the pushes and pulls your body is making. Hold a tug of war.
Drama	-	Act out what may happen in a road accident.
R.E.	-	Talk about feelings when a favourite toy is lost or broken.

TALK ABOUT

- what happens when we push or pull objects.
- the word 'force'.
- what makes some toys speed up, slow down and change direction.
- what happens to real cars in accidents.
- what happens to people who are accidentally run over.
- toy cars running down ramps.
- magnetic forces.
- types of vehicles to be made.
- size and shape of chassis to be used.
- shape, size and materials for wheels.
- which tools are to be used.
- which joinings are to be used.
- the cool glue gun and its benefits.
- keeping safe.
- the order in which work is to be carried out.

ACTIVITIES

Experiment with:
Moving a brick with/without rollers - toy cars running down a ramp - toy cars running into plasticine people - floating and sinking - running against the wind with a large flat board - pushing a balloon under water - pushing and pulling with a magnet.

Build a moving toy based on a plank chassis. Pupils should be introduced to the variety of plank chassis that it is possible for them to make. Pupils should choose one bearing in mind the type of vehicle they have decided to make after discussion, looking at books, pictures and visits.

Build the chassis and test how well it works - improve if necessary. Pupils should choose own junk materials to be joined onto their chassis.

Complete the model finishing appropriately.

Test the model and improve its performance.

STARTING POINTS

A collection of pupils' moving toys.

Pupils can disassemble simple vehicles to discover how axles and wheels are connected. Talk about the shape of wheels, size etc.

Make observations of the moving parts of toys.

Pupils should be taught in small groups and individually how to correctly use a junior hacksaw and vice or bench hook.

Listen to poems about vehicles e.g. 'The wheels on the bus'.

Useful Books
Finding Out About Things That Go - Pub. Usborne.
The "Gumdrop" Series by Val Biro - (The Adventures of a Vintage Car) - Pub. Hodder and Stoughton.
Cars, Boats and Planes - Richard Scarry etc.

RESOURCES/EQUIPMENT

Wood, corriflute, card, box bases.
Screw eyes, clip clothes pegs, cable clips, plastic tubing, card triangles.
Dowel, wheels, cool glue gun, saws, rice, bench hooks.
Junk materials.
String.

Possible Visits
A toy museum; an interactive museum such as Eureka; a garage/fire station/railway station; 'Toys-R-Us'.

Possible Visitors
Policeman/Fireman/Mechanic to talk about their work with vehicles.

Best Time of Year
Summer term if vehicles are to be tested outside.

Moving Toys

ART AND DISPLAY

Make a display of moving toys; past and present; toys for very young children; toy trains; toy cars; dolls; toys featured in children's books etc.

Use the display for observational drawing, painting or collage work.

Make an observational drawing in which you modify, alter or change the original. Can friends spot the difference?

Combine different features from several toy cars/dolls to design a new one.

Note the colours used for toys for very young children - collect and use these in a design of your own.

Look at moving toys that have become the focus of stories e.g. Thomas the Tank Engine. Paint, draw or collage a picture of your own 'toy' character and write a story about it.

DIRECTED PLAY

Sand and Water
Introduction of water/sand wheels for use in sand and water trays. Children to investigate moving parts (axles). Junk materials placed in trays to discover suitability of materials e.g. plastic, card, wood.

Role Play
On a bus, on a train, on a plane. Make rows of seats. Sell tickets, drinks, food etc.

Imaginative Play
Model town play with road map, fire engines, police cars, ambulances, buses, houses, building sites, railway etc.

Play with Constructional Toys
Construction kits that demonstrate wheel and axle connections in Duplo, Mobilo, Toolo etc.

END PRODUCT

Pupils to show the vehicles they have created at assembly.

Testing of vehicles - pushing down a slope etc. Measure distances travelled and directions moved in. Talk about fair tests. Predict and test improvements to be made.

Make a transport frieze with different examples of moving vehicles.

Make a 3D mock up of a toy shop window.

Write simple reports and make drawings of models constructed.

PROGRAMME OF STUDY

The quality of the environment in any locality, either in the United Kingdom or overseas, should be investigated.

Pupils should be taught:
- to express views on the attractive and unattractive features, e.g. *tidiness, noise*, of the environment concerned, e.g. *a play area, a street, a small area of woodland*
- how that environment is changing, e.g. *increasing traffic*
- how the quality of that environment can be sustained and improved, e.g. *creating cycle lanes, excluding cars from an area.*

SKILLS TO BE DEVELOPED

- observe, question and record, and to communicate ideas and information
- use geographical terms, e.g. hill, river, road, in exploring their surroundings
- undertake fieldwork activities in the locality of the school e.g. observing housing types, mapping the school playground
- follow directions, including the terms up, down, on, under, behind, in front of, near, far, left, right, north, south, east, west
- make maps and plans of real and imaginary places, using pictures and symbols, e.g. a pictorial map of a place featured in a story, a plan of their route from home to school
- use globes, maps and plans at a variety of scales; the work should include identifying major geographical features, e.g. seas, rivers, cities, locating and naming on a map the constituent countries of the United Kingdom, marking on a map approximately where they live, and following a route
- use secondary sources, e.g. pictures, photographs (including aerial photographs), books, videos, CD-ROM encyclopaedia, to obtain geographical information

SUPPORTING CURRICULUM LINKS

English - Poetry based on adjectives stimulated by an environment studied.

Maths - Compare temperatures of different environments.

Science - Study animal homes e.g. Pond Visit.

History - Present children with a photograph of the locality and a bank of comments to sort into FACT or OPINION e.g. This is a nice place/ There is a green hill.

Music - Compose music which evokes the mood of a particular locality e.g. green fields/bustling shops.

R.E. Element: Ask the question "Do people wear different clothes according to the environment they are in e.g. clothes for on the beach; on a skiing holiday; doing sport; going to work." Do some clothes show different types of work? e.g. policeman, fireman, clergyman, Salvation Army member etc. Why do clergymen dress as they do? Do other people dress differently for worship? e.g. Jews, Sikhs etc. How do we show our love and care for the environment?

TALK ABOUT

- what can be found in a wood?
- what can be found in a pond?
- what can be found in our street?
- what can be found in a shopping street?
- why are things there?
- what do they do?
- how do things change?
- who cares for things?
- how can we improve the environment?
- how can we protect the environment?
- what is our responsibility?
- what do we like about this place?
- what do we not like about it?
- what makes a place attractive?
- things you could do in this place
- what does it feel like to be in this place?
- improving our home environment
- improving our school environment

ACTIVITIES

Mark on a map of the U.K.; where they live, this locality, other localities studied, England, N. Ireland, Scotland, Wales etc.

Likes/Dislikes list for locality.

Each group work on a different idea for improving the locality and produce a group plan: drawing, list of equipment needed, jobs needed to be done etc. (e.g. a pond, a nature area, vegetable garden, litter clean up etc.)

Plan a new play area for the locality.

"How to look after..." Large peacock on the wall. Each child is given a peacock feather to write how to sustain and improve the environment of the locality (e.g. create a cycle lane), creating a colourful peacock of ideas.

Look at 2 photos of the locality and list changes that have taken place.

Linked to science: create an "ideal" community in space - what rules would you make so that your new environment would be protected and enhanced?

STARTING POINTS

Talk about "Our Environment" being the surroundings in which we live. Talk about shopping/work/play/school/home environments. Choose two contrasting environments to study. (This work maybe linked to a farm/zoo/park/countryside visit/pond visit etc.)

Look at photographs of the locality - discuss what they can see.

Label a large photograph of the locality with geographical terms e.g. hill, river, road etc.

Mark the exact location of the locality on a local map (if close by) or a regional or U.K. map.

Useful Books
'Dinosaurs and all that Rubbish' - Michael Foreman.
'Giant' - Juliet and Charles Snap.
'The World that Jack Built' - Ruth Brown.
'The Town Mouse and The Country Mouse".

RESOURCES/EQUIPMENT

From the locality: Maps/plans/photos (recent and historical) of the locality.
Aerial photos.
Posters.
Weather measuring kit.
'Photocopiable Pond Activity Book - Pub. by Topical Resources.

Possible Visits
This "environmental study" could be local and therefore a visit may be possible.

Possible Visitors
Council Planners/Parks and Gardens Department Workers.
Vet - needs of small animals like the school hamster.

Best Time of Year
If the locality is close by good weather may be needed, otherwise anytime.

What is an Environment?

ART AND DISPLAY

Display pictures of the place which you plan to visit.

Take photographs during the visit to use on display and as a later stimulus for drawing, painting etc.

Collect e.g. on a park visit, leaves, twigs, pebbles etc. and make a display box or collage of them on your return.

Junk model of the bus, canal boat, tractor etc.

Clay model of buildings/animals seen.

Quick sketches could be made on the visit and developed later.

Choose a motif e.g. leaf/animal/fish to use as a border motif in cut paper or printing as a border around writing about the visit.

Draw a series of pictures to show the sequence of the visit. Make a map. Make an illustrated brochure of the place visited to encourage others to visit.

DIRECTED PLAY

Sand and Water
Experiment with rain (watering can) coming down on sand hills. Where does the water always end up? Does it form puddles or lakes?

Role Play
Two contrasting areas/environments during the study to compare e.g. a woodland scene with animal masks and then a busy train station booking office in a city.

Imaginative Play
Different environments to explore:
- cars and buses on city streets
- create a winding country lane with fields and animals.

Play with Constructional Toys
Design a cleaning machine to keep the streets clean and safe.

END PRODUCT

Each group produces a large scale pictorial map showing improvements they would make to the area.

Tapes of interviews with local people expressing their ideas about improving the locality: interviewed by the children.

Display of children's likes and dislikes; written on separate cards (possibly word processed).

Produce a ten point plan for improving the locality and make it into a video like a local T.V. report.

Class display of small animal homes (designed in D & T).

Time-line of changes made to the locality - with photographs as the environment changes/improves.

PROGRAMME OF STUDY

Pupils should be taught:
- the differences between things that are living and things that have never been alive
- that animals, move, feed, grow, use their senses and reproduce
- that plants need light and water to grow
- to recognise and name the leaf, flower, stem and root of a flowering plant
- that flowering plants grow and produce seeds which, in turn, produce new plants
- that living things can be grouped according to observable similarities and differences
- that there are different kinds of plants and animals in the local environment
- that there are differences between local environments and that these affect which animals and plants are found there
- to design and make their own products
- to take apart simple manufactured products to learn how they function; assess the quality of a product; consider safety at all times and use appropriate vocabulary for equipment, materials and components used.

SKILLS TO BE DEVELOPED

- to turn ideas suggested to them, and their own ideas, into a form that can be investigated
- to think about what is expected to happen when planning what to do
- to recognise when a test or comparison is unfair
- to explore using appropriate senses
- to make and record observations and measurements
- to communicate what happened during their work
- to use drawings, tables and bar charts to present results
- to make simple comparisons
- to use results to draw conclusions
- to indicate whether the evidence collected supports any prediction made
- to try to explain what they found out

When Designing - generate, discuss and develop ideas; communicate designs through sketches and models; improve original ideas and decide how to proceed.

When Making - select tools; measure, mark out, cut and shape materials; assemble, join and combine materials and components; finish off and evaluate the product.

SUPPORTING CURRICULUM LINKS

English	-	Listen to stories and poems about animals and plants e.g. 'Five Little Speckled Frogs', 'Jack and the Beanstalk' etc.
Maths	-	Measure the growth of plants and display in bar charts. Make sets of flowers according to similarities and differences using observable features.
I.T.	-	Use simple wordprocessors to create text for pop up life-cycle books.
History	-	Make a time chart which shows the sequence of events in the life of a tree.
Geography	-	Make simple maps of a local environment or one visited during the study.
R.E.	-	Talk about the importance of caring for living things.

TALK ABOUT

- which things are alive and which have never been alive.
- what is a plant
- the names of several different kinds of plants.
- the different parts of a plant.
- conditions plants need to grow and reproduce.
- the life-cycle of a plant e.g. bean.
- animals that are pets.
- animals found on a farm
- animals found in a zoo.
- animals found in the wild in this country.
- the type of environment frogs are found in.
- conditions a frog needs to grow and reproduce.
- the life-cycle of a frog.
- a variety of pop-up books.
- how a pop up book works.
- what to include in a pop-up book which shows the life-cycle of a bean.
- what to include in a pop-up book which shows the life-cycle of a frog.

ACTIVITIES

Experiment with winged seeds. Make your own from paper.

Collect seeds and sort by hard/fleshy cases.

Disect and examine bulbs. Watch and record growth in water.

Plant cress on a variety of surfaces e.g. soil, gravel, damp cotton wool, bark etc. Observe growth in different conditions.

Observe and record growth of tadpoles.

Observe and record growth of beans.

Take apart teacher made pop-up cards that demonstrate V and opening mouth cuts. Pupils should experiment with and discuss actual book.

Make group books to demonstrate the life-cycle of a frog which contain pop-up techniques.

Take apart teacher made or commercial cards and books to demonstrate sliding taps.

Groups create sliding tab pictures to demonstrate the growing seeds.

STARTING POINTS

Walk around the local environment - list, sketch, photograph, collect evidence of plants and animals.

Story - Jack and the Beanstalk - plant beans in jam jar with water and blotting paper.

Collecting frogspawn and placing it in a natural made habitat - record the progress made.

Useful Books

Chicken and Egg - Stopwatch series - Pub. by A & C Black.
My Class Visits a Park - Pub. by Franklin Watts.
Young Scientist Investigates - Seeds and Seedlings - Pub. by Oxford Books.
The photocopiable Pond Book - Pub. by Topical Resources.

RESOURCES/EQUIPMENT

Fish tank and materials to naturalise it.
Clear plastic containers, blotting paper, plant pots, seeds, card, a variety of equipment for cutting and joining card, felt tips, word processor etc.

Possible Visits

Garden Centre; Florist; Park; Farm; Zoo; Bird Reserve; Wild Life Park etc.

Possible Visitors

Local environment group e.g. National Parks; a vet; farmer; zoo keeper; nurseryman; R.S.P.C.A. worker; dog/cat breeder; pets and their young.

Best Time of Year

Spring/Early Summer.

iving Things

ART AND DISPLAY

Display a collage of living/non-living items.

Record cress/bean/tadpole growth as a sequence of drawings.

Make leaf prints in the colours of the leaf e.g. different greens, reds, browns etc. Cut up the most successful bits into squares to make a colour family patchwork.

Use pets/minibeasts for observational drawing.

In 3D make a model pet in clay - design an imaginary minibeast/plant from junk materials.

Look at Georgia O'Keefe flower paintings from your own observational drawings of flower work.

Display animals/plants depicted by different artists including photographs.

Look at and draw in large scale the patterns on e.g. bean seeds, ladybirds etc. Develop a pattern using silhouette, or by printing e.g. butterflies, flowers, fish.

DIRECTED PLAY

Sand and Water
Use diggers and lorries to dig pits for model zoo animals. Create a model zoo in the sand.

Role Play
Setting up the house corner as a garden centre/greenhouse. Feeding, watering and transplanting the seedlings etc.

Imaginative Play
Farm play with various animals and animal transporters. Zoo play with different animals and pens.

Play with Constructional Toys/Sheet Materials
Experiment with a wide variety of card, paper, old greetings cards, glues and cutting equipment to perfect the techniques introduced.

END PRODUCT

Sandwiches made from the grown cress.

Planting of mature seedlings into school garden or tubs around the school to improve the local environment.

Easter cards of opening mouth technique, sliding tab, could be a chicken or a frog or a bunch of flowers - pupils use suggested ideas and turn them into their own card.

Books on developing tadpoles and plants to be placed in school/class library - protect with sticky backed plastic.

Simple reports of experiments observed.

Drawings and explanations of pop-up and moving cards made.

PROGRAMME OF STUDY

Pupils should be taught:
- to investigate changes in the lives of their family or adults around them
- about the everyday life, work, leisure and culture of men, women and children in the past, e.g. clothes, diet, everyday objects, houses, shops and other buildings, jobs, transport, entertainment.

At "Story" and "Assembly" times:
Pupils should be taught about the lives of different kinds of famous men and women, including personalities drawn from British history, e.g. rulers, saints, artists, engineers, explorers, inventors, pioneers.
Pupils should be taught about past events of different types, including events from the history of Britain, e.g. notable local and national events, events in other countries, events that have been remembered and commemorated by succeeding generations, such as centenaries, religious festivals, anniversaries, the Gunpowder Plot, the Olympic Games.

SKILLS TO BE DEVELOPED

- to be able to sequence events and objects, in order to develop a sense of chronology
- to be able to use common words and phrases relating to the passing of time e.g. old, new, before, after, long ago, days of the week, months and years
  to be able to investigate aspects of the past through stories from different periods and cultures, including stories and eyewitnesses accounts of historical events
- to be able to recognise why people did things, why events happened and what happened as a result
- to be able to identify differences between ways of life at different times
- to be able to identify different ways in which the past is represented e.g. pictures, written accounts, films, plays, songs, replica objects and museum displays
- to be able to find out about aspects of the past from a range of sources of information, including artefacts, pictures and photographs, adults talking about their own past, written sources, and buildings and sites
- to ask and answer questions about the past.

SUPPORTING CURRICULUM LINKS

English	-	Design a questionnaire asking about childhood. Tape interviews. Collect a bank of family memories.
Maths	-	Venn diagrams of games we play/ parents played/grandparents played.
Technology	-	Research and design a psychadelic tie.
Geography	-	Compare maps of now and in 1950's.
Music	-	Learn popular songs from 1950's. Learn playground skipping rhymes.

R.E. Element: Listen to different versions of the first man and woman story from Christian/Jewish/Muslim traditions. Talk about people who choose to live alone and those that take a partner. Play a class game where one child is left out - talk about how they feel. Talk about: what is a family?; what makes a house a home?; a time you have been alone; what it would be like to live alone; older family members that have recently set up their own home; why people choose to live together; weddings the children have attended; weddings from Christian/Jewish/Islamic traditions; Gran and Grandad's wedding.

TALK ABOUT

- life before T.V.

- listening to the radio

- how 'we' could write and make our own radio broadcast

- the pros and cons of having a T.V.

- food when Gran and Grandad were young

- Italian/Indian/Chinese food

- food rationing

- how homes were heated

- life without central heating

- household machines

- popular holidays e.g. Holiday camps, Wakes weeks etc.

- shopping and the first supermarkets

- decimalisation of coins.

ACTIVITIES

Family Time-Lines,Family/Generation Trees.

Large - scale time - line in class for events. Children research/photographs brought in etc.

Provide 3 artefacts on the same theme (e.g. carpet beater, Eubank, Vacuum) - sequence them, sketch them, describe them and then add the appropriate one to role play area.

Use information books/library books to research a particular aspect of life in the 1950's (e.g. clothes, shops, transport, entertainment).

Examine school log books for evidence of subjects studied, punishments received in school at that time.

Watch a Pathe News Broadcast on video and work as a group to produce a simple newspaper front cover for that day.

Ask the children, parents and grandparents to write about a day at the seaside as a child: clothes, activities, food, transport, cost, games, sun protection etc.

Compare the responses.

STARTING POINTS

Invite Grans and Grandads in to chat to the class informally or be interviewed about their early life.

Present the children with an old photo to explore/discuss.

Ask a grandparent to write a letter to the children asking them to find out as much as they can about the 1950's for his/her family history book giving the children a sense of purpose.

Useful Books
Grandpa - John Burmingham.
My Grandma has black hair - Hoffman & Burroughs Methuen.
Our Gran - A Sense of History (Longman).
Gran and Grandpa - Helen Oxenbury.
Grandpa Pearson - Letitia Parr.
Even Granny was Young Once - E Janikovsky.
The Patchwork Quilt - Valerie Flournoy.
At School in the 1950's ed Sallie Purks (Into the Past Longman).

RESOURCES/EQUIPMENT

Reference books for children/comics, slides, posters, magazines, clothes, newspapers, music, photos from the period.

BBC TV Video - Watch with mother
Pathe News Videos of the period
Artefacts/clothing from museum service or collected locally,

Possible Visits
Local Museum - check with the Education Officer whether they run workshops on this period or artefact sessions.
Local newspaper office to examine newspapers from the period.

Possible Visitors
Grans and Grandads.
Museum Education Officer.

Best Time of Year
Any

When Gran & Grandad Were Young

ART AND DISPLAY

Collect and display photographs, books, clothes, items of interest from the time.
Let children dress in appropriate clothes - then use them as a focus for drawing and painting.
Draw everyday objects e.g. an old valve radio, shoes, hats etc with a modern equivalent.
Collect pictures of cars and houses of the era and use as a stimulus for junk modelling.
Make travel posters for the same destination in the styles of 'now' and 'then',
Draw a series of pictures which show/describe a pastime popular at the time.
Examine packaging which has remained the same e.g. Bird's Custard. Use for observational drawing, pattern or colour work.

DIRECTED PLAY

Sand and Water
Use the water area to create a 1950's wash day! Wash clothes using a wash board and soap etc.

Role Play
Make a 1950's living room at the time of the coronation (an occasion which brought TV to many homes for the first time). Equip with appropriate dressing up clothes, record player and furniture.

Imaginative Play
Play games grandparents played. (eg hoola hoop, marbles etc).

Play with Constructional Toys
Design a machine that would make life easier in the home. (eg a bed maker/washing pegger outer/self mowing grass etc...).
Play with 1950's construction kit (eg Minibricks or steel strip meccano).

END PRODUCT

Create your own family fact-file with data about your family members (age, height, pastimes, favourite food etc).

Fifties exhibition - ask grandparents to loan exhibits and invite them in to be shown around.

Display photographs of grandparents and the children's descriptions - can you match them up?

"Grandparents Assembly" - invite grandparents in to a school assembly during which the class can share their findings with everyone.

1950's fashion show with children and parents modelling clothes worn by Gran/Grandad when they were young.

Invite grandparents in to teach games they played to the children (hopscotch, ludo, hula hoop etc...)

Hold a 1950's day in class: all the children dress appropriately, listen to popular music, are taught to twist or waltz and hold a 1950's disco that evening for families.

PROGRAMME OF STUDY

Pupils should be taught:
- that objects made from some materials can be changed in shape by processes including squashing, bending, twisting and stretching
- to describe the way some everyday materials, e.g. water, chocolate, bread, clay, change when they are heated or cooled
- to design and make their own products
- to take apart simple manufactured products to learn how they function; assess the quality of a product; consider safety at all times and use appropriate vocabulary for equipment, materials and components used.

SKILLS TO BE DEVELOPED

- to turn ideas suggested to them, and their own ideas, into a form that can be investigated
- to think about what is expected to happen when planning what to do
- to recognise when a test or comparison is unfair
- to explore using appropriate senses
- to make and record observations and measurements
- to communicate what happened during their work
- to use drawings, tables and bar charts to present results
- to make simple comparisons
- to use results to draw conclusions
- to indicate whether the evidence collected supports any prediction made
- to try to explain what they found out

When Designing - generate, discuss and develop ideas; communicate designs through sketches and models; improve original ideas and decide how to proceed.

When Making - select tools; measure, mark out, cut and shape materials; assemble, join and combine materials and components; finish off and evaluate the product.

SUPPORTING CURRICULUM LINKS

English	-	Write a story about a Gingerbread man. Make up imaginary recipes to turn people into.....! Write down a favourite recipe from home. Make up a class recipe book as a present for parents. Plan and carry out a survey of favourite school dinners.
Maths	-	Money and weighing in the shop. The time of day we eat. Make charts of favourite foods. Measure liquids for baking. Name shapes of food packaging.
History	-	Traditional English food. How food was cooked before electricity and gas.
Geography	-	Foods from other cultures. Look at maps to find where food comes from and how it gets to us.
R.E.	-	What is a vegetarian? Which religious traditions does this involve? Make up/collect a book of graces. Listen to stories from the Bible which include food such as the "Loaves and Fishes".

TALK ABOUT

- words to describe different types of bread colour, shape, texture and taste.
- why the baker wears specialist clothing.
- how a windmill/cornmill works; the process from corn to flour.
- what happens to water when heated.
- what happens to water when cooled.
- what happens to an egg when it is boiled.
- how we get meat and fish.
- food that comes from farms.
- healthy food and unhealthy food.
- good manners and how to set a table.
- why we keep food in cans.
- why we keep food in a fridge.
- the changes which occur whilst cooking a packet of soup.

ACTIVITIES

Taste different types of bread. Make individual assessments as to likes and dislikes.

Bake bread in small groups. Compare and contrast the effects of different types of sandwich fillings. Make up new combinations. Make sandwiches for a class picnic.

Make butter (from cream shaken up).

Examine a variety of foods under a binocular microscope or other magnifiers. Draw results.

Dissolve foods e.g. salt, sugar, flour etc.

Taste foods and group as sweet, sour, salt or bitter.

Mix boiled red cabbage water with lemon juice, tea, sugar and vinegar - observe colour changes.

Heat ice, water, wax and chocolate and observe the results.

Compare white, brown and castor sugar.

Grind corn in the classroom.

STARTING POINTS

Learn rhymes/listen to stories about food e.g. Pat-a-cake, Pat-a-cake; Oats and beans and barley grown.

Visit a local bakery to see how bread is made.

Visit a bakers shop and talk about different types of bread.

Visit a local supermarket in groups to purchase a variety of flours, fats, dry and fresh yeast.

Buy different types of bread and taste them.

Bake bread in school.

Useful Books
Collins Primary Technology KS1 Set "Pat-a-cake, Pat-a-cake".
My Class Enjoy Cooking - Thompson - Pub. by Franklin Watts.
Topsy and Tim Can Cook - Blackie.
The Little Red Hen - Ladybird Books.
The Very Hungry Caterpillar - E. Carle Pub. by Hamish Hamilton.
A Packet of Poems - J. Bennet Pub. by O.U.P.

RESOURCES/EQUIPMENT

A wide variety of baking utensils including tins and trays for different shaped breads.
Bread ingredients.
Binocular microscope; various magnifiers; small cooker; pans etc.

Possible Visits
Local bakery and shops to see types of bread; farm; dairy; school kitchen etc.

Possible Visitors
Local baker into school to bake bread varieties with children.
School cook; farmer; milkman etc. to talk about their work.

Best Time of Year
Any - ties in well with harvest.

Food Glorious Food

ART AND DISPLAY

Draw cross-sections of fruit and vegetables - use these shapes as a starting point for pattern work.

Make a collection of foods of similar colours and use for colour/observational drawing and painting.

Make a collection of textured food e.g. cauliflower, melon, onion, orange, bread etc. Describe the textures.

Make salt dough/papier mache models of fruit and veg. - colour match when painting.

Draw an orange cross-section but paint in unusual colours.

Make a 3D meal described in a story e.g. The Twits. Design an alternative meal of a similar type.

Look at artists who depict food/meals in their paintings in different ways e.g. Renoir, Cezanne, Andy Warhol, Claus Oldenburg etc.

Illustrate and describe how to make your favourite meal.

DIRECTED PLAY

Sand and Water
Bread tins etc. placed in the sand tray - wet sand and dry sand - when will it mould from the tins?

Role Play
Turn the house corner into a bakers shop. Make loaves, baps etc. from salt dough, varnish with watered pva and the loaves will remain hard for months. Play with money.

Imaginative Play
Farm play with model dairy farm with milk tanker - dolls tea party with modelled food.

Play with Constructional Toys/Mouldable Materials
Salt dough, playdoh, soff mo, plasticine etc.

END PRODUCT

Loaves of bread baked and eaten with a variety of fillings to make sandwiches.

Class assembly of the story of "A loaf of bread" or "A pint of milk".

Plan and carry out a small class party.

Prepare and serve a meal for some invited guests.

Devise a food tasting quiz to carry out on others.

Take part in a religious festival which gives thanks for the harvesting of food.

Simple reports of experiments observed.

Drawings and explanations telling how bread was made and the sandwich fillings used.

PROGRAMME OF STUDY

Pupils should study a locality, either in the United Kingdom or overseas, in which the physical and/or human features contrast with those in the locality of the school. The locality of the school is its immediate vicinity; it includes the school buildings and grounds and the surrounding area within easy access. The contrasting locality should be an area of similar size.

Pupils should be taught:
- about the main physical and human features, e.g. *rivers, hill, factories, shops*, that give the localities their character.
- how localities may be similar and how they may differ, e.g. *both areas may have farmland, but animals may be kept on the farms in one area, while in the other crops may be grown*
- about the effects of weather on people and their surroundings, e.g. *the effect of seasonal variations in temperature on the clothes people wear*
- how land and buildings, e.g. *farms, parks, factories, houses*, are used.

SKILLS TO BE DEVELOPED

- observe, question and record, and to communicate ideas and information
- use geographical terms, e.g. *hill, river, road*, in exploring their surroundings
- undertake fieldwork activities in the locality of the school, e.g. *observing housing types, mapping the school playground*
- follow directions, including the terms up, down, on, under, behind, in front of, near, far, left, right, north, south, east, west
- make maps and plans of real and imaginary places, using pictures and symbols, e.g. *a pictorial map of a place featured in a story, a plan of their route from home to school*
- use globes, maps and plans at a variety of scales; the work should include identifying major geographical features, e.g. *seas, rivers, cities*, locating and naming on a map the constituent countries of the United Kingdom, marking on a map approximately where they live, and following a route
- use secondary sources, e.g. *pictures, photographs (including aerial photographs), books, videos*, CD-ROM encyclopaedia, to obtain geographical information.

SUPPORTING CURRICULUM LINKS

English	-	Produce their own passport.
Maths	-	Venn diagram of transport used on holiday.
Technology	-	Design and make a sun hat or sun glasses. Plan a holiday picnic/long cool drink.
I.T.	-	Word process labels for own holiday luggage.
History	-	Examine Victorian seaside scenes for similarity and difference.

R.E. Element: Talk about what a journey is; different types of journeys made; journeys the children have been on; types of transport used; feelings before/ during/after journeys e.g. on holiday; reasons for journeys. Listen to some of the journeys made in the Bible. Talk about special journeys called Pilgrimages. Find out about Christian Pilgrimages to Lordes or The Vatican; Muslim Pilgrimages to Mecca etc. Talk about "Holidays = Holy Days". Discuss holy days at home and in other cultures.

TALK ABOUT

- The children's experience of holidays - where? when? how? who with? what did you do? see? my best holiday?

- Holiday brochures and what they are used for. Focus in on a specific locality. Activities can be used to answer the questions.

- What is this place like?

- Where is this place?

- Why is this place as it is?

- How is this place connected to other places?

- How has this place changed?

- How is this place changing?

- What does it feel like to be in this place?

ACTIVITIES

Sort postcards/photos of children's holidays into boxes of different categories e.g. seaside/countryside/town.

Photos and postcards of the locality to sort into shoe boxes of different categories e.g. seashore/town/ houses/hills/countryside/shops/factories etc.

List similarities and differences between features of the locality and their own immediate area. Look at locality photos old and new.

Using information provided (e.g. photos/children's letters/tourist info. etc.) draw own pictorial map of what you think the resort looks like.

Which jobs could you do in the locality? Compile a class list (or gather information from the link school) and compare with i.e. occupations of our families.

Visitor's book: Children write a comment about the locality (i.e. likes and dislikes) in a "visitor's book" and sign it.

STARTING POINTS

Talk about where the children have been on holiday.

Collect postcards/holiday photos and display on a map in class.

Discuss how their holiday destination is similar to/ different from home.

Focus in on a specific "holiday" locality which can then be used as the focus for the activities that follow.

Useful Books
Fiction -
Dear Daddy - Philippe Dupasquier.
Spot Goes on Holiday - Eric Hill.
Bear Goes to Town - Anthony Browne.
Teddybears Take the Train - Susanna Gretz and Alison Sage.

RESOURCES/EQUIPMENT

From the locality: Maps/plans/photographs (recent and historical)/postcards/tourist information packs/school link in the locality? Aerial photographs. Simple world/ map/globe/atlas and maps of the U.K.

Possible Visits
Travel Agents.
Airport/port/railway station.
U.K. contrasting locality.

Possible Visitors
Travel Agent.
Visitor to the locality who has returned.
Visitor from the locality for children to interview.

Best Time of Year
Autumn term, following long summerbreak.

On Holiday

ART AND DISPLAY

Display holiday brochures, tickets, souvenirs etc.

Display different types of luggage e.g. suitcase, rucksack, picnic baskets etc. Use for observational drawing.

Design a simple eye-catching label to help you identify your luggage.

Make an illustrated brochure of an 'imaginary' holiday destination showing the things you would like to see there - this could be in collage form made from old holiday brochures.

Make a 3D model of a holiday resort.

Draw clothes for a winter/summer holiday.

Design a postcard to send home.

Make a log of a family beach/countryside holiday.

Collect holiday souvenirs - use for drawing.

Design a souvenir for where you live.

DIRECTED PLAY

Sand and Water
Turn sand and water tray into a beach resort.
Children bring in equipment and toys they would take to the beach. Play with wet sand to make sandcastles - exploring shapes/sizes. Use water tray as floating area - what floats/sinks. Capacity with buckets etc.

Role Play
Travel Agents - Airport Check-In Desk - Aeroplane.

Imaginative Play
Harbour/Airport/Train Station - make buildings/ vehicles/landscape features and enact scenes seen in photographs.

Play with Constructional Toys
Make transporters to take you on holiday in the future. Make cranes/ships/planes/aircraft etc.

END PRODUCT

Produce a video about your own locality to swap with a school in the contrasting locality

A holiday advertisement for the locality based on the information provided.

A holiday brochure for the locality.

A taped interview with someone from the locality or someone who has visited the locality.

A letter to a child in the locality or their local Tourist Information Centre requesting information about the locality.

Take the class on an imaginary journey: pack suitcases/ stamp passports/fly in a plane/unpack at hotel/relax on beach (particularly good for dance and drama).

PROGRAMME OF STUDY

Pupils should be taught:
- that many everyday appliances use electricity
- to construct simple circuits involving batteries, wires, bulbs and buzzers
- that electrical devices will not work if there is a break in the circuit
- that light comes from a variety of sources, including the Sun
- that darkness is the absence of light
- that there are many kinds of sound and many sources of sound
- that sounds travel away from sources, getting fainter as they do so
- that sounds are heard when they enter the ear
- to design and make their own products
- to take apart simple manufactured products to learn how they function; assess the quality of a product; consider safety at all times and use appropriate vocabulary for equipment, materials and components used.

SKILLS TO BE DEVELOPED

- to turn ideas suggested to them, and their own ideas, into a form that can be investigated
- to think about what is expected to happen when planning what to do
- to recognise when a test or comparison is unfair
- to explore using appropriate senses
- to make and record observations and measurements
- to communicate what happened during their work
- to use drawings, tables and bar charts to present results
- to make simple comparisons
- to use results to draw conclusions
- to indicate whether the evidence collected supports any prediction made
- to try to explain what they found out

When Designing - generate, discuss and develop ideas; communicate designs through sketches and models; improve original ideas and decide how to proceed.

When Making - select tools; measure, mark out, cut and shape materials; assemble, join and combine materials and components; finish off and evaluate the product.

SUPPORTING CURRICULUM LINKS

English	-	Write a description of a candle burning. Listen to a piece of music and write about your feelings afterwards. Write secret messages using mirror writing.
Maths	-	Make symmetrical shapes using mirrors. Use shadow puppets for number rhymes and games e.g. 10 in the bed.
History	-	Interview older members of the community about the coming of electricity.
Geography	-	Talk about how the sun gives us day and night.
I.T.	-	Play with Lego Control Box.
P.E.	-	Experiment with human shadows outside on a sunny day.
Music	-	Explore how to make sounds by plucking, shaking, scraping and blowing using familiar objects and simple musical instruments.
R.E.	-	Find out why and when candles are used in church services. Consider "light and dark" feelings.

TALK ABOUT

- everyday appliances that use electricity.
- the dangers from 'high powered electricity' such as in the home and from car batteries.
- safe batteries found in torches and toys.
- sources of light including the sun.
- the difference between light and dark.
- how we can light bulbs with simple circuits.
- how to make simple shadows.
- reflections.
- which things reflect and which do not.
- different ways of making sounds.
- sounds made by a variety of instruments.
- how sound travels through the air.
- that ears are designed to detect sounds.
- how far away you have to stand before you can not hear sounds.

ACTIVITIES

Take apart a bicycle bell and a simple household plug - emphasise DANGERS of doing this at home!

Light up a bulb with a battery and two wires.

Make a buzzer work with a battery and two wires.

Make a bell work with a battery and two wires.

Add a simple switch to each of above.

Light a bulb with a battery and three wires.

Draw the circuits they have made.

Construct a lighthouse using junk materials. Fit it with a working light. Make it flash by creating breaks in the circuit.

Light the rooms in a dolls house. (Dolls house can be teacher/class made or a bought one.)

Create a face with eyes that light up, a nose that rings, a mouth that buzzes and a bow tie that spins.

STARTING POINTS

Talk about safety in the home, things that are worked by electricity and the dangers of touching plugs and sockets.

Talk about sources of light in and around the home and school.

Collect pictures of light sources - lamps, bulbs, the sun etc. Make a collage of light sources.

Listen to stories about light houses.

Take apart a torch - examine what elements it is made up of.

Make a collection of children's toys which use batteries.

Useful Books

Science with Light and Mirrors - Usborne.
Science with Batteries - Usborne.
Electricity and Magnetism - Topical Resources.
Light and Sound - Topical Resources.
Making Shadow Puppets - Leisure Craft 30 - Pub. Herder and Herder.

RESOURCES/EQUIPMENT

Wire, bulbs, batteries, motors, buzzers, electric bells, wire cutters etc.
Dolls house, junk materials etc.
Coloured cellophane, card.
A variety of cutting and joining equipment and materials.
Magazines, torches, appropriate percussion instruments etc.

Possible Visits

A factory which makes lamps or light bulbs etc.
A shop which sells a variety of light sources.
Puppet exhibition in museum.

Possible Visitors

Health and Safety Officer from the Police or Fire Service.

Best Time of Year

Any.

Batteries, Bulbs, Bells & Buzzers

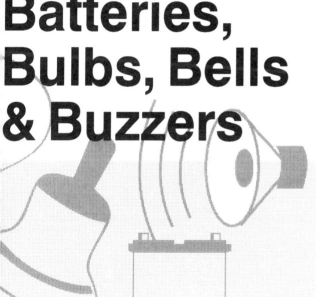

ART AND DISPLAY

Make a collection of pictures of different types of bells and display with bells from music trolley.

Use pictures and bells for observational drawing.

Collect different sizes and shapes of bulbs - cut out silhouettes of one shape and use for pattern work. Draw the inside of a bulb.

Draw the inside of a bicycle bell.

Use colours and lego on a battery for colour matching and enlarging work - e.g. look at part of design and scale up.

Design an unusual bell for the front door of a dentist, plumber, builder etc.

Draw toys that have bells attached to amuse very young children or pets - design a new version of your own.

Study pictures and then draw a clowns face - later develop into a toy which will buzz, ring or light up. Can you make a rotating bow tie?

DIRECTED PLAY

Sand and Water
Dry sand trickled, dropped onto taught surfaces e.g. drum, tight plastic over a coffee tin etc.

Water ripples, waves (compare to sound waves).

Role Play
Make role play area into shadow puppet theatre - sell tickets, sweets, ice-cream, drinks etc. Seat the audience, perform a play, bring in next "house"!

Imaginative Play
Free play with musical instruments.
Free play with various torches.

Play with Constructional Toys
Lego and the Lego Control Box and the sound, light and motor elements.

END PRODUCT

Make a game which includes a circuit that could be used at a school fete.

Make simple circuits by following drawings made by other children.

Make safety posters for display around the school and in the local library.

Tell a story in school assembly using shadow puppets. Use as many sound effects, lighting effects and musical instruments as possible.

Make up individual booklets of children's work including reports from experiments carried out, stories written and designs for models.

PROGRAMME OF STUDY

Pupils should be taught:
- about the way of life of people in Britain in the past beyond living memory
- about the everyday life, work, leisure and culture of men, women and children in the past, e.g. clothes, diet, everyday objects, houses shops and other buildings, jobs, transport, entertainment.

At "Story" and "Assembly" times:
Pupils should be taught about the lives of different kinds of famous men and women, including personalities drawn from British history, e.g. rulers, saints, artists, engineers, explorers, inventors, pioneers.
Pupils should be taught about past events of different types, including events from the history of Britain, e.g. notable local and national events, events in other countries, events that have been remembered and commemorated by succeeding generations, such as centenaries, religious festivals, anniversaries, the Gunpowder Plot, the Olympic Games.

SKILLS TO BE DEVELOPED

- to be able to sequence events and objects, in order to develop a sense of chronology
- to be able to use common words and phrases relating to the passing of time e.g. old, new, before, after, long ago, days of the week, months and years
- to be able to investigate aspects of the past through stories from different periods and cultures, including stories and eyewitnesses accounts of historical events
- to be able to recognise why people did things, why events happened and what happened as a result
- to be able to identify differences between ways of life at different times
- to be able to identify different ways in which the past is represented e.g. pictures, written accounts, films, plays, songs, replica objects and museum displays
- to be able to find out about aspects of the past from a range of sources of information, including artefacts, pictures and photographs, adults talking about their own past, written sources, and buildings and sites
- to ask and answer questions about the past.

SUPPORTING CURRICULUM LINKS

English	-	Each child write about his/her adventures as a knight.
Maths	-	Measure width of castle walls on castle visit.
Science	-	Look for evidence of weathering on castle visit.
Technology	-	Design and build a model draw bridge.
I.T.	-	Draw a floor plan of a castle. Children program roamer to visit different rooms.
Geography	-	Draw room plans.
Music	-	Listen to medieval music.

R.E. Element: Find out about "A day in the life of a monk." Talk about: what he would wear; why he chose to live such a life; a typical day; his home; how he helps in the community; the importance of prayer. Invite a monk (or local priest/clergyman) to talk about how they dress. Make a "Day in the Life" booklet with pictures and simple sentences. Practice sitting quietly for short periods of time. Talk about the thoughts which went through your mind. Find out about modern monks and monks from traditions other than Christianity e.g. Buddhism.

TALK ABOUT

- Myths and legends with castle settings such as King Arthur.
- Why, when, where, how castles were built.
- Who lived in them?
- The work the inhabitants did.
- The food they ate.
- How they dressed.
- How they entertained themselves.
- How comfortable life was inside the castle.
- Living in a castle under siege.
- Why castles fall into disrepair by talking about what would happen to the school if left unattended for hundreds of years.
- How it feels to wear armour (best if a child can actually be dressed in period armour).

ACTIVITIES

Create a time-line for the castle with photos or drawings where possible.
Sequence different photos/drawings of the castle.
Complete a NOW AND THEN SIMILARITY AND DIFFERENCE list for 2 pictures.
(e.g. medieval and today's ruin)
(e.g. medieval and today restored and extended castle)
Prepare an invitation and menu for a feast in the Grand Hall.
Draw up a defence plan for the school and draw parallels between this and castle defences. Which elements are still intact? Which have disappeared?
Each group explore a different aspect of the castle and produce a 'Fun-Fax' style 'Info-Pack' for the rest of the class. Sections could include: Defences/Domestic Arrangements/Lords and Knights/Entertainment/Dress etc.
Design a "Castle of the Future" with fast-food lazer shows, leisure facilities etc.

STARTING POINTS

Start with a story: lots of popular fairy tales include castles (e.g. Cinderella, Rapunzel). Ask the children to draw what they think a castle looks like.

Compare with posters/photographs/drawings and story book castles (e.g. Disney).

Visit a local castle. Compile a list of questions the children would like answering about a castle. Display them and seek to answer them in the course of this unit of work.

Useful Books
English Heritage: A Teacher's Guide to using a Castle.
Food and Cooking in Medieval Britain.
Eyewitness: Castle (Doring Kindersley).
Castle - Francesa Baines.
What were castles for? (starting points history).
Castles - Topic Box Series (Wayland).
Castles, Pyramids and Palaces - Beginners Knowledge Series (Usborne).
Sir Cedric: Roy Gerrard.

RESOURCES/EQUIPMENT

Education packs from local museums.
Model castle packs.
Re-production armour from museums.
'Music of the Age of Chivalry' from History in Evidence, Chesterfield.

Possible Visits
Local castles.
Local museum - check with Museum Education Officer whether they run workshops/artefact sessions about this period.

Possible Visitors
Museum Education Officer.

Best Time of Year
Summer term or when weather is suitable for a visit to a castle.

Life in a Castle -
many years ago

ART AND DISPLAY

Look at paintings of castles, e.g. by John Piper and draw/paint a castle in a similar style.

Make a 3D model of a ruined castle.

Cut paper designs could be produced using the portcullis - window shapes - battlements etc. as a stimulus.

Make a black and white silhouette of a castle with a sunset behind.

Design a flag for your castle or a banner for inside.

Make a 3D model in clay of a suit of armour - cover in tin foil.

Make in clay/salt dough the food for a banquet.

Look carefully at the costumes worn by knights pages/servants/ladies of the castle. Draw yourself dressed as one of them.

Design a shield for you to use.

Make in junk - a sword - a ring/necklace/chain - a headress/hat/helmet that might have been worn.

DIRECTED PLAY

Sand and Water
Make a model castle with a moat. Hold a sandcastle design and construction competition.

Role Play
Turn the role play area into a "mini" banqueting hall or castle kitchen. Hold a feast with your friends.

Imaginative Play
Play with model castle (possibly one the class has made). Explore different bridges and their strengths.

Play with Constructional Toys
Build castles with different construction kits.
Design a working drawbridge using a kit.

END PRODUCT

A giant floor model of a castle. Large scale display of work.

A medieval day with appropriate dress, music, activity and ending in a family medieval evening with food, jesters, musicians etc. (This could even take place in the grounds of a local castle or ruin!)

Each group or table prepare its own joisting colours, emblem and flag and make shields etc. to hang over their desks.

Produce a class guide book for the castle you have visited or the imaginary castle created in the classroom.

Knights (i.e. the children) write and swear on oath of Allegiance to the Lord and the castle (i.e. the school).

PROGRAMME OF STUDY

Pupils should be taught:
- to design and make simple products
- carry out practical tasks in which they develop and practice particular skills and knowledge (in this case - how the working characteristics of materials relate to the ways materials are used)
- take part in activities in which they investigate, disassemble and evaluate simple products
- work with a range of materials and components
- work independently and in teams
- apply skills, knowledge and understanding from other subjects e.g. The following is from the science prog.:
- about friction, including air resistance, as a force which slows moving objects
- that when springs and elastic bands are stretched they exert a force on whatever is stretching them
- that when springs are compressed they exert a force on whatever is compressing them
- that unbalanced forces can make things speed up e.g. *an apple being dropped*, slow down, e.g. *shoe sliding across the floor*, or change direction, e.g. *a ball being hit by a boat*.

SKILLS TO BE DEVELOPED

Designing Skills
- generate ideas
- clarify ideas and suggest ways foward
- consider appearance, function, safety and reliability
- model ideas to explore aspects of the design
- evaluate design ideas and look for improvements
- develop a clear idea of what has to be done

Making Skills
- select appropriate materials, tools and techniques
- measure, mark out, cut and shape a range of materials using appropriate tools and equipment
- join and combine materials and components accurately in temporary and permanent ways
- apply finishing techniques appropriate to the purpose of the product
- evaluate the product by carrying out appropriate tests
- implement improvements identified as being necessary

SUPPORTING CURRICULUM LINKS

English	-	Creative Writing - e.g. A trip in a hot air balloon/Chitty Chitty Bang Bang/Time Machine etc.
Science	-	Testing forces, friction and motion.
History	-	Research history of transport.
Geography	-	Research kites/windmills from around the world.
Music	-	Explore sounds made from elastic bands.
P.E.	-	Movement - balancing, starting/stopping, increasing/decreasing speed.

WHOLE CLASS ACTIVITIES

Revisit plank chassis with variety of axle fittings. Disassemble a strip and dowel chassis.

Teach how to build a strip and dowel chassis. Teach how to build a chassis using Jink's triangles. Demonstrate sails made from black bin bags, hot air balloons powered by a hair dryer, gliders made from expanded polystyrene, models powered by elastic bands etc.

Make temporary models using temporary fixings and/or construction kits of windmills, kites, hot air balloons, gliders, land-yachts etc.

Experiment with ways to improve the model e.g. does changing the shape of sails make windmills run faster?

Make temporary models which use elastic bands, springs, pneumatics and hydraulics as a source of power. Again, experiment with ways to improve.

SMALL GROUP ACTIVITIES

Decide which of the moving models they are going to create in permanent ways in groups.

Discuss ways in which the model may be constructed.

Individually draw designs.

Debate with an adult and the rest of the group the best design points to be used.

Finalise the design.

Allocate tasks and collect appropriate materials.

Build the moving model.

Test the model and look for improvements.

Build improvements into model.

STARTING POINTS

Discuss and examine models which make use of air e.g. windmills, kites, hot air balloons, gliders, land yachts etc.

Discuss and examine models which make use of elastic bands, springs, pneumatics and hydraulics e.g. cotton reel tanks, bagatels etc. Talk about how power is stored up.

Talk about the forces involved in a moving cotton reel tank. Talk about unbalanced forces on a snooker table. Demonstrate.

Look at books which show how to make moving models.

Recommended Reference Books
The Know How Book of Action Toys - Usborne
The Know How Book of Action Games - Usborne
How to Make - Paper Superplanes - Usborne
How to Make - Kites - Usborne

RESOURCES/EQUIPMENT

String, plastic bags, plastic cups, springs, elastic bands, fabric, parachute silk, sticky tape, strip wood, dowel, wheels, syringes, plastic tubing.
Flexible sheet materials - card, plastic, tissue, paper.
Construction kits - Lasy, Lego, Bauplay etc.

Possible Visits
Local industry, factories or museums.

Possible Visitors
Hot air balloon enthusiast!

Best Time of Year
Any

Design and Make: Moving Models
(forces and motion)

ART AND DISPLAY

Design a shape/logo/pattern for a hot air balloon.

Weave a basket/decorate a box for a model balloon.

Design a car/lorry/bus body for a vehicle of the future.

Display pictures/drawings/famous works (e.g. Van Gogh, Mondrian) of different windmills including from different parts of the world.

Display observational drawings of kites or people flying kites using photographs as a stimulus.

Draw a design of a kite looking at tails, colours, shapes, decorations etc.

INDIVIDUAL ACTIVITIES

Make designs in sketch books using annotated drawings.

Select appropriate materials.

Select appropriate tools.

Practice making skills with the tools and materials.

Participate in the construction of the model.

Draw simple diagrams which show forces involved on a snooker table.

Make your own model windmill, kite, hot air balloon, glider, land-yacht, elastic band powered vehicle, cotton reel tank etc.

Build a model powered by an electric motor.

END PRODUCT

A working model of a: windmill, kite, hot air balloon, landyacht etc.

A working model of an elastic band powered glider, model car, truck or bus etc.

A working model of a moving bridge, railway signal, tipping truck etc.

A sketch book containing ideas, drawings and photographs of designs and models.

A cotton reel tank competition to see which model will travel the furthest distance.

A display of all models completed with sketches showing processes gone through.

PROGRAMME OF STUDY

The locality of the school should be studied. At this key stage this should cover an area larger than the school's immediate vicinity. It will normally contain the homes of the majority of pupils in the school.
Pupils should be taught:
- about the main physical and human features
- how this locality may be similar and how it may differ from another
- how the features of a locality influence the nature and location of human activities within it
- about recent and proposed changes in the locality
- how the locality is set within a broader geographical context and linked with other places
In studying how settlements differ and change, pupils should be taught:
- that settlements, e.g. villages, towns, cities, vary in size and that their characteristics and locations reflect the types of economic activities in the settlement, e.g. market towns, ports, seaside resorts
- how land in settlements is used in different ways, e.g. for housing, transport, industry
- about a particular issue arising from the way land is used e.g. different groups of residents in a settlement have conflicting views on the construction of a by-pass across farmland.

SKILLS TO BE DEVELOPED

- observe and question about geographical features and issues, collect/record evidence to answer questions, analyse, draw conclusions and communicate findings
- use appropriate geographical vocabulary to describe and interpret their surroundings
- undertake fieldwork using appropriate instruments
- make maps and plans at a variety of scales
- use and interpret globes, and maps and plans at a variety of scales; the work should include using co-ordinates and four-figure grid references, measuring direction and distance, following routes, using the contents page and index of an atlas, and identifying the points of reference specified on the Geog. N.C. maps
- use secondary sources of evidence to provide information e.g. pictures; photographs (including aerial photographs) T.V.; radio; books; newspapers; visitors
- use IT to gain access to additional information sources and to assist in handling, classifying and presenting evidence.

SUPPORTING CURRICULUM LINKS

English	-	Debate environmental issues such as using local transport instead of individual cars. Compose a letter to the local council with suggestions for improving your area.
Maths	-	Work on four-figure co-ordinates.
Science	-	Research how electricity is made and how it gets into people's homes.
I.T.	-	Make a data base of the different types of homes children in the class live in.
History	-	Investigate the history of your locality.
Music	-	Use maps and local newspapers to find places to enjoy live music.
P.E.	-	Orienteering exercises.
R.E.	-	Talk about a "sense of community". Find out about children and adults that live on the streets in cities throughout the world.

WHOLE CLASS ACTIVITIES

Talk about the advantages/disadvantages of living close to others.

Talk about the physical features that make a good settlement site e.g. water/food supply, defence etc.

Talk about the human requirements of a modern settlement e.g. house/shops/work etc.

Discuss the main occupations in your locality - which are common to other locations, which are distinct e.g. port/car factory/farming etc.

Investigate a recent or new development in your area e.g. motorway/factory construction. Debate the issues involved.

Talk about transport and the problems of traffic pollution. Make proposals to improve the situation.

Learn about scale, map symbols and co-ordinates.

Learn how to use a compass and simple maps. Go orienteering in the school grounds.

SMALL GROUP ACTIVITIES

Talk about and list your likes and dislikes about your locality. Design an improvement e.g. new park, playground, sports complex etc.

List the requirements of your ideal home. Then investigate using local papers/estate agents details the nearest to the ideal you can purchase for fixed amounts e.g. 50/75/100/150/200 thousand pounds.

Make a map of the area around your school showing different types of land use.

Compare old and new maps of the same area to discover changes which have taken place. Give reasons for the changes.

Use maps to help you list similarities and differences between your area and another.

Compare aerial photographs with large scale maps of the same area. List features you can find on both.

STARTING POINTS

Plan and build a model settlement. Include a shopping centre, roads, church, cinema, factory buildings and various types of housing. If space allows include a small airport and dock. Ask children to bring in appropriate "matchbox" vehicles, roughly the correct scale.

Use the model to talk about the "ingredients" of a settlement e.g. housing, shops, work places etc.

Discuss and research the definitions of hamlet, village, town, suburb, city, conurbation and decide which category your community come into.

Make a survey (or go and examine) the land use in your community e.g. housing, shopping, farming, industry, leisure etc.

Recommended Reference Books
Charlie and the Chocolate Factory (Industrial Awareness) - R. Dahl - Puffin.
The Town - Watson & King - Usborne Books.
How a Town Works - Howard - Macdonald Educational.
Britain - Maps & Mapwork - Macmillan Education.
Settlements - Wayland.
Where I Live Series - Watts Books.

RESOURCES/EQUIPMENT

I.T. - Mapventure - Geography and Mapping Skills - Sherston Software.
P.C.E.T. wall chart - The Built Environment, Structures and Materials, What is a Map?, Maps and Scale, Mapping the Street.
A class set of atlases which can be used to locate your village, town or city.
A selection of large scale maps of the area e.g. local street maps; O.S. 1" series, 1:2500, 1:10000 etc. A selection of local postcards, directories, local history books, aerial photographs etc.

Possible Visits
Local council chambers; local trading estate; housing estate; shopping centre; leisure centre etc.
A local high point to "look down on your community".
A local industry to see how a raw material is turned into a useful product.

Possible Visitors
Town planner; the Mayor; businessman; fireman; health visitor etc. to talk about "their patch".

Best Time of Year
Any.

Village, Town or City?
(a settlement study)

INDIVIDUAL ACTIVITIES

Make a list of the services a settlement needs e.g. electricity supply, postman, sewers, police, firemen etc.

Design a public open space.

Write your address including the earth, solar system etc.

Locate your locality on national and international maps.

Design a tram or other public transport system of the future.

Compare maps of different scales but of the same area.

Draw/paint pictures which illustrate local land use.

Make a collection of pictures of an environment different from your own.

Make a map with symbols and a key of your route to school.

Use four figure grid references to locate features on a local map.

ART AND DISPLAY

Make a collection of photographs of old/new buildings plus buildings of importance in the locality.

Model/draw/paint using these as a stimulus.

Make a collection of drawings of door ways - cut out shapes of different windows, gates, chimney pots and use for pattern work.

Design a new set of street signs in a different style.

Look at paintings, by different artists of villages, towns, cities in different parts of the world past and present.

Look at different architectural styles and attempt to find some in your locality.

Draw/paint/model your favourite place locally.

Make a model of a local street with a 2D background and 3D people, vehicles etc. Make a model of a local park.

END PRODUCT

A class model of a fictious (or partially factual) town/city which includes roads, airport, docks, railway, various types of housing, shopping areas, churches, industry and services e.g. police, fire, hospital, garages, cinema etc.

A collage showing examples of local land use in action amidst appropriate natural features.

Individual topic booklet containing stories written and information collected.

A quiz based on a large scale street map of your area.

A large scale map containing as much detail and information about your local area as possible.

A collection of posters to advertise improvements to the area e.g. anti-litter, park and ride, neighbourhood watch etc.

PROGRAMME OF STUDY

Pupils should be taught:
- that light travels from a source
- that light cannot pass through some materials, and that this leads to the formation of shadows
- that light is reflected from surfaces, e g mirrors, polished metals
- that we see light sources, e.g. light bulbs, candles, because light from them enters our eyes
- that sounds are made when objects, e.g. strings on musical instruments, vibrate but that vibrations are not always directly visible
- that the pitch and loudness of sounds produced by some vibrating objects, e.g. a drum skin, a plucked string, can be changed
- that vibrations from sound sources can travel through a variety of materials, e.g. metals, wood, glass, air, to the ear.

SKILLS TO BE DEVELOPED

- to be able to turn ideas suggested to them, and their own ideas, into a form that can be investigated
- to know that making predictions can be useful when planning what to do
  to decide what evidence should be collected
- to know that changing one factor and observing and measuring the effect, whilst keeping other factors the same, allows a fair test or comparison to be made
- to consider what apparatus and equipment to use
- to use simple apparatus and equipment correctly
- to make careful observations and measurements
- to check observations and measurements by repeating them
- to use tables, bar charts and line graphs to present results
- to make comparisons and to identify trends or patterns in results
- to use results to draw conclusions
- to indicate whether the evidence collected supports any prediction made
- to try to explain conclusions in terms of scientific knowledge and understanding

SUPPORTING CURRICULUM LINKS

English	-	Write poems about colour, fire works, etc. Discuss pleasant and unpleasant sounds from various points of view e.g. neighbour and loud music; motorsport and nearby houses etc.
Maths	-	Measure angles light is reflected from a plane mirror
History	-	Research the invention of the telephone or the electric light
Geography	-	Research the causes of thunder and lightning
Music	-	Listen to a wide variety of instruments
P.E.	-	Exercise making shadows on the playground
R.E.	-	Find out about the Jewish festival of Hanukah; Advent rings; Christingle services and why electric lights are used on Christmas trees.

WHOLE CLASS ACTIVITIES

Talk about how the eye sees objects, how the ear hears sounds and how the mouth makes sounds.

Discuss the different sources of light including the sun.

Discuss materials light will/will not shine through.

Define the terms transparent, translucent and opaque.

Demonstrate how a prism can be used to split light.

Demonstrate how to make shadow puppets.

Examine a collection of musical instruments and talk about how sounds are made by plucking, shaking, blowing, banging and twanging.

Demonstrate how a vibrating tuning fork makes sounds. Investigate what happens when a vibrating tuning fork comes into contact with various materials including water and a ping-pong ball suspended on a length of cotton thread.

Investigate ways of making different sounds with the musical instruments.

SMALL GROUP ACTIVITIES

Experiment with:
Images made with different combinations of mirrors.
Images made on curved surfaces such as bendy plastic mirrors or shiny objects such as spoons.
Lenses of different sizes and shapes.
Light passing through different shaped containers filled with water.
Tall objects stood in a jar filled with water.
Colour mixing with a torch and coloured cellophane.
Spinning wheels with coloured patterns.
Shadows made from different light sources.
Different sounds made by plucking stretched materials, shaking loose objects, blowing over bottles or striking different materials.
How pitch and loudness can be changed.
Sounds passing through different materials.
Distances sounds travel.
Simple aids for listening to sounds.

STARTING POINTS

List sounds heard in the classroom and outside.
Make a collection of musical instruments.
Listen to a variety of music - discuss likes and dislikes.
Make simple shadow puppets and experiment with them.
Make shadows with hand shapes and different objects.
Make a collection of shiny objects.
Make a simple circuit to light a bulb.

Recommended Reference Books
Oxford Young Scientist Investigates - "Light and Colour" and "Sounds" - Oxford University Press.

"Science with Light and Mirrors" - Usborne.

Bang and Rattle, Blow and Puff, Pluck and Scrape, Squeak and Roar - 4 books - Pub. by Watts.

Light and Sound - Photocopiable Experiments - Topical Resources.

RESOURCES/EQUIPMENT

Safe plastic mirrors; various hand lenses including concave and convex; coloured filters; prisms; torch etc.

P.C.E.T. Wallcharts "Communication, Light and Colour" and "Making Musical Instruments."

I.T. - Music Box - Topologika Software.

Possible Visits
The Theatre to see use of coloured lights to "create atmosphere" and listen to live music.

Possible Visitors
A travelling puppet theatre group. A lighting technician - lighthouse keeper - musician - peripatetic music teacher.

Best Time of Year
Any.

Light & Sound

ART AND DISPLAY

Collect pictures of the same view at different times of the day. Look at Monet's series paintings e.g. Rouen cathedral painted at different times of day and in different weather conditions.
Make observational drawings of part of school at different times of day and under different weather conditions.
Draw different light sources - candles in candlesticks - torches - old fashioned style lamps. Make a collection of these for display.
Consider tonal work - light and dark, colour work - light and dark.
Collect a colour family of dark blue - light blue. Look at artists who use colour and shape to interpret sounds - Georgia O'Keefe Blue and Green Music - Mondrian Broadway Boogie Woogie.
Paint a pattern/abstract in similar style based on e.g. red and yellow music - in response to music - high and low sounds - playground sounds etc.
Paint a colour or shape for the sounds of individual musical instruments - use in a design/abstract composition. Draw and paint musical instruments.

INDIVIDUAL ACTIVITIES

Design and make a string telephone.
Design and make a simple periscope.
Design and make musical instruments from junk materials.
Design and make individual shadow puppets.
Write a simple play or find a children's story to use puppets with.
Research the speed of light and sound. Attempt to compare with everyday moving objects.
Draw and paint a large detailed picture of your own eye using a mirror.
Send secret messages using mirror writing.
Make flick books to make pictures move.
Make list of words with similar sounds.

END PRODUCT

Build a shadow theatre and perform a play for the rest of the school. Try to include coloured lighting and appropriate sound effects.

Make up individual topic booklets containing reports from experiments, information collected, stories written etc.

Class talk by small group with hand out telling of what they found out in their investigation.

Hold a sound quiz. Perform a musical concert with home-made instruments. Hold a musical talent concert. Produce a musical play.

PROGRAMME OF STUDY

Pupils should be taught in outline about the following:
- the Roman conquest and occupation of Britain
- the arrival and settlement of the Anglo-Saxons
- Viking raids and settlements

They should be taught in greater depth about:
- the arrival and settlement of the Anglo-Saxons and their impact on England, e.g. *early settlement, the conversion of the Anglo-Saxons to Christianity, King Alfred and Anglo-Saxon resistance to the Vikings*
- everyday life, e.g. *houses and homelife, work, religion*
- the legacy of settlement, e.g. *place names and settlement patterns, myths and legends, Anglo-Saxon remains, including artefacts and buildings.*

SKILLS TO BE DEVELOPED

- to be able to place events, people and changes in periods studied within a chronological framework
- to be able to use dates and terms relating to the passing of time, including ancient, modern, BC, AD, century and decade
- to have an understanding of the characteristic features of particular periods and societies
- to be able to describe and identify reasons for and the results of main events and changes in the periods studied and make links across periods
- to be able to identify and give reasons for different ways in which the past is represented and interpreted
- to be able to find out about aspects of the periods studied from a range of sources of information including documents and printed sources, artefacts, pictures and photographs, music and buildings and sites
- to know the terms necessary to describe the periods and topics studied, including court, monarch, parliament, nation, civilisations, invasion, conquest, settlement, conversion, slavery, trade, industry, law.

SUPPORTING CURRICULUM LINKS

English	-	Write: A day in the life of an Anglo-Saxon farmer or monk. Listen to the story of King Alfred and the cakes. Debate whether fact or fiction. Make up Anglo-Saxon riddles. Learn stories to "tell" the rest of the class.
Maths	-	Make circle patterns and turn them into designs for jewellery.
Science	-	Experiment with different ways of joining wood to use for the sides of model cottages.
Technology	-	Design and make working models of Saxon carts or simple water mills.
Geography	-	Look for Anglo-Saxon place names on a map (e.g. dene=hill, ford=river crossing, ham=settlement, leigh= clearing in the woods, worth=land enclosed by a hedge).
R.E.	-	Investigate Anglo-Saxon pagon Gods and how Christianity finally spread across Britain.

WHOLE CLASS ACTIVITIES

Make a time line through history showing when the Anglo-Saxons invaded Britain.

Make a time line of important events in Anglo-Saxon Britain.

Talk about who the Anglo-Saxons were, their place of origin and why they came to Britain.

Listen to stories about the Legend of King Arthur.

Debate if stories true or not.

Define the terms Thanes, Churls and Slaves.

Map the seven Anglo-Saxon Kingdoms.

Learn about Offas Dyke.

Discuss what evidence is available to us to help build up a picture of the Anglo-Saxon way of life e.g. the Sutton Hoo treasure discovered in Suffolk in 1938.

Discuss the two different types of Christianity which spread across Britain and the Whitby Synod of 664.

Make a class model of an Anglo-Saxon family settlement complete with church, hall, cottages, roads and farmland.

SMALL GROUP ACTIVITIES

Construct a full size Anglo-Saxon soldier in battle dress.

Design illuminated letter shapes.

Write passages from the Bible in manuscript form with quill and ink.

Act the part of archaeologists and examine a bag of artefacts e.g. sword, shoe, cloak, plate, jewellery etc. Speculate who owned these objects and how they lived.

Research and make a calendar of seasonal jobs to do on the farm.

Discuss the uses of artefacts shown in pictures.

Make a map showing where the Angles and Saxons came from.

Design and make a support to hold a cooking pan over an open fire.

Write messages to each other using letters from the Futhork (Anglo-Saxon alphabet).

STARTING POINTS

Talk about the Roman conquest and occupation of Britain; the arrival and settlement of the Anglo-Saxons; Viking raids and settlements. Then focus on the Anglo-Saxons.

Listen to the story of Beowulf.

Listen to a class novel set in Anglo-Saxon times e.g. 'The Lantern Bearers' by Rosemary Sutcliff.

Visit to a local museum to look for evidence of Anglo-Saxon presence in the area.

Dress in simple cloaks with sword and shield - act out a battle scene.

Build an Anglo-Saxon model village with accurately constructed cottages.

Recommended Reference Books
From Cavemen to Vikings - R.J. Unstead - Pub. by A & C Black.
The Anglo-Saxons Activity Book - British Museum Publications.
The Saxons and the Normans - Paperbird.
The Anglo-Saxons - BBC Factfinders.

RESOURCES/EQUIPMENT

A collection of Anglo-Saxon artefacts or reproduction everyday items from Museum Service.

Examples of reproduction Anglo-Saxon dress.

I.T. - Archaeology - open-ended computer program about an archaeological dig - Cambridgeshire, Software House.

Philip Green A4 picture pack - Saxons and Vikings.

P.C.E.T. wallchart - The Anglo-Saxons.

Possible Visits
Local museum to look for Anglo-Saxon remains.
Local church with evidence of Anglo-Saxon remains.
Offa's Dyke. West Stow Country Pack and Anglo-Saxon Village.

Possible Visitors
Curator or Education Officer from museum.
Amateur archaeologist.

Best Time of Year
Any.

nvaders & settlers: Anglo Saxons

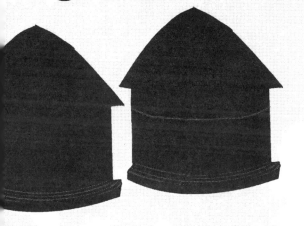

ART AND DISPLAY

Look at Celtic designs - Mythical beasts - illuminated letters - the Book of Kells.

Draw an imaginary mythical beast based on a familiar animal.

Make an interlocking celtic design in cut paper shapes and collect pictures, e.g. of celtic jewellery, around and popular today.

Write your own name. Illuminate the first letter.

Paint a picture of yourself in Anglo-Saxon costume.

Explore weaving using different materials and threads - include threads coloured by using natural materials, e.g. beetroot.

Design an Anglo-Saxon cross - or use the designs on one to produce a pattern of your own.

INDIVIDUAL ACTIVITIES

List the differences between rich and poor Anglo-Saxon cottages.

Research one aspect of Anglo-Saxon life e.g. food, types of farming, fishing, pottery, trade etc.

Research Anglo-Saxon town and village names still used today.

Research 'The Alfred Jewel'. Design your own with a personal message inscribed.

Research how to make linen cloth.

Make Anglo-Saxon dress for 'Barbie' type dolls.

Make an individual contribution for the class model of a farming settlement.

Make a reproduction model helmet.

Make reproduction swords and shields.

Make jewellery from clay.

Design a woollen cloak for export by a trader.

END PRODUCT

Construct a menu of typical Anglo-Saxon food, shop and hold a feast. Make/listen to appropriate music and tell stories and poems for entertainment.

Make up individual topic booklets containing stories written and information collected.

Display of model village typical of the time.

Display of model cottages showing "tongue and groove" type wooden walls and thatched roofs.

Large Time Line showing where Anglo-Saxons are found in British history.

Time Line showing main events of Anglo-Saxons times.

PROGRAMME OF STUDY

Pupils should be taught in outline about the following:
- the Roman conquest and occupation of Britain
- the arrival and settlement of the Anglo-Saxons
- Viking raids and settlements

They should be taught in greater depth about:
- Viking raids and settlement and their impact on the British Isles, e.g. their settlement in different parts of the British Isles, King Alfred and Anglo-Saxon resistance to the Vikings
- everyday life, e.g. houses and home life, work, religion
- the legacy of settlement, e.g. place names and settlement patterns, myths and legends, Viking remains, including artefacts and buildings.

SKILLS TO BE DEVELOPED

- to be able to place events, people and changes in periods studied within a chronological framework
- to be able to use dates and terms relating to the passing of time, including ancient, modern, BC, AD, century and decade
- to have an understanding of the characteristic features of particular periods and societies
- to be able to describe and identify reasons for and the results of main events and changes in the periods studied and make links across periods
- to be able to identify and give reasons for different ways in which the past is represented and interpreted
- to be able to find out about aspects of the periods studied from a range of sources of information including documents and printed sources, artefacts, pictures and photographs, music and buildings and sites
- to know the terms necessary to describe the periods and topics studied, including court, monarch, parliament, nation, civilisations, invasion, conquest, settlement, conversion, slavery, trade, industry, law.

SUPPORTING CURRICULUM LINKS

English	-	Write: A visit to a Viking market. The first Viking raid on Lindisfarne from (i) a Viking point of view (ii) a monk's point of view. A day in the life of a Viking boy. A Viking warrior's diary. A Viking poem or saga.
Maths	-	Measure out the size of a Viking longboat on the school playground.
Science	-	Experiment with different materials and mixtures to make wattle and daub walls.
Technology	-	Design and build a model Viking loom. Use it to weave some cloth.
Geography	-	Use maps to discover Viking place names e.g. _____ toft, _____ thwaite, _____ thorpe etc.
R.E.	-	Talk about Viking burial mounds and the sort of things found in them and question why! Discuss Viking Gods and how we know they eventually became Christian.

WHOLE CLASS ACTIVITIES

Make a time line through history showing when the Vikings invaded Britain.

Make a time line of important events in Viking Britain.

Find out about the laws made by King Alfred.

Talk about the first Viking raid on Lindisfarne.

Talk about why the Vikings came; how they conquered; the peace made with King Alfred.

Find out about everyday life in Britain under the Vikings including: Viking houses; dress; food; pastimes; occupations; etc.

Define the term trade. Make maps showing routes taken by Vikings to trade with other countries.

Learn about the importance of Sorrik.

Find the meaning of Danelaw and Danegeld.

Discuss what evidence is available to us to help build up a picture of the Viking way of life e.g. stone crosses in church yards, farmstead ruins, Viking treasure, everyday artefacts, Jorvik, place names etc.

SMALL GROUP ACTIVITIES

Dress a child in Viking costume or armour for others to sketch.

Model part of a Viking settlement. Combine with other groups to make a class model.

Make a full size mock-up of a Viking warrior complete with armour and weapons.

Send runic messages to each other.

Make up memorial stone inscriptions using runes.

Carve runes on slabs of clay.

Examine the finds from a pretend archaeological dig (e.g. costume jewellery, comb, pieces of material, old shoe, coins, cups, bowls, buckets etc.). Speculate about what sort of person would have used these items.

Devise a set of instructions with diagrams telling how to build a full size longship.

Construct a map of Viking occupied land in Britain.

Research and draw a plan of a typical Viking settlement.

STARTING POINTS

Talk about the Roman conquest and occupation of Britain; the arrival and settlement of the Anglo-Saxons; Viking raids and settlements. Then focus on the Vikings.

Listen to a class novel set in Viking times e.g. 'Axe Age, Wolf Age' by Kelvin Crosley Holland or 'Viking Dawn' and other stories by Henry Treece.

Visit to local museum to look for evidence of Viking presence in the area.

Act out a Viking raid on a British settlement.

Discuss their reasons for these actions.

Recreate a Viking saga in a school play.

Recommended Reference Books
From Cavemen to Vikings - R.J. Unstead - Pub. by A & C Black.
The Vikings - Stanier and Sutton - Pub. by BBC Books in association with Heritage Books.
The Vikings Activity Book - D.M. Wilson - British Museum Publications.
The Vikings - S. Barton - Ladybird Books.

RESOURCES/EQUIPMENT

Local museum loan of artefacts or replicas.

I.T. - Adventure III ... The Vikings - An archaelogical adventure into the age of the Vikings - Sherston Software.

BBC Zig Zag - 5 programmes on the Vikings.

Philip Green A4 picture pack - Saxons and Vikings.

P.C.E.T. wallchart - Vikings.

Usborne model to construct "Viking Settlement".

Possible Visits
Local Viking remains - the best being the Jorvik Viking Centre in York. A local museum may have some Viking remains in their collection.

Possible Visitors
Curator or Education Officer from museum.
Amateur archaeologist.

Best Time of Year
Any.

Invaders & settlers:
Vikings

ART AND DISPLAY

Look at Norse Legends illustrated e.g. by Michael Foreman - illustrate part of your own Norse Legend.

Look at Ancient Scandinavian design - draw a strange animal - bird in a similar design.

Make a large scale collage of a Viking face - or a clay tile of one.

Look at the designs on Viking coins - design one in clay.

Design a dragons head shape for the front of a Viking boat. Use several of these shapes to make a pattern.

Make a model boat complete with clay figures.

Make brooches/necklaces/rings using the design of Viking jewellery in your own way.

Junk model a Viking helmet.

INDIVIDUAL ACTIVITIES

Make sketches of Viking tools and implements.

Make models of Viking trading and fighting ships.

Make copies of Viking jewellery.

Make clay models of Viking chessmen and learn how to play the game.

Research one aspect of Viking life e.g. sports/pastimes/Norse Gods and legends.

Make a full size copy of a Viking dagger, spear, sword or shield.

Make copies of Viking memorial stones.

Draw a cross-section of a Viking longboat and label the parts.

Design and make a Viking shoe from junk materials.

END PRODUCT

Research appropriate foods, devise a menu, shop and hold a Viking feast.

Make up individual topic booklets containing stories written and information collected.

Display a model of a Viking settlement complete with longships in the harbour.

Large Time Line showing when in History the Vikings came to Britain.

Large maps showing Viking voyages of exploration and settlement.

A Viking Saga acted out for school and parents.

Large pictures of men and women depicting typical dress and family life.

PROGRAMME OF STUDY

Pupils should be taught in outline about the following:
- the Roman conquest and occupation of Britain
- the arrival and settlement of the Anglo-Saxons
- Viking raids and settlements

They should be taught in greater depth about;
the Roman conquest and its impact on Britain e.g.
*Boudicca and resistance to Roman rule, the extent to
which life in Celtic Britain was influenced by Roman
rule and settlement, the end of imperial rule*
- everyday life, e.g. houses and home life, work, religion
- the legacy of Roman rule, e.g. *place names and
settlement patterns, Roman remains, including
artefacts, roads and buildings.*

SKILLS TO BE DEVELOPED

- to be able to place events, people and changes in periods studied within a chronological framework
- to be able to use dates and terms relating to the passing of time, including ancient, modern, BC, AD, century and decade
- to have an understanding of the characteristic features of particular periods and societies
- to be able to describe and identify reasons for and the results of main events and changes in the periods studied and make links across periods
- to be able to identify and give reasons for different ways in which the past is represented and interpreted
- to be able to find out about aspects of the periods studied from a range of sources of information including documents and printed sources, artefacts, pictures and photographs, music and buildings and sites
- to know the terms necessary to describe the periods and topics studied, including court, monarch, parliament, nation, civilisations, invasion, conquest, settlement, conversion, slavery, trade, industry, law.

SUPPORTING CURRICULUM LINKS

English	-	Write poems about battle. Write a letter home from a soldier serving on Hadrian's wall telling of the terrible conditions. Write about a visit to a Roman villa; bath house; theatre; chariot race. Write from a Roman or British point of view. Listen to the story of Romulus and Remus and discuss if fact or fiction. Find out how the Romans gave us the names of our months.
Maths	-	Work with Roman numbers and Roman currency.
Science	-	Experiment with everyday items buried during the length of the topic - which do/do not change.
Technology	-	Design and construct a working model of a Roman aquaduct.
Geography	-	Use maps to study the extent of the Roman Empire and the routes taken by Roman roads in Britain.
P.E.	-	Practice marching with Roman swords and shields. Devise defensive positions.
R.E.	-	Investigate Roman Gods and how Christianity was brought to Britain.

WHOLE CLASS ACTIVITIES

Make a time line through history showing when the Romans invaded Britain.

Make a time line of main events in Roman Britain.

Talk about life in Britain before the Romans.

Talk about why the Romans came, how they conquered and the fact they they created settlements.

Learn the story of Boudicca; the make up of the Roman army and how the British hill forts were defeated.

Find out about everyday life in Britain under the Romans including: Roman Towns, Roads, Baths, Houses, Food, Dress, School and Religious Beliefs.

Discuss what evidence is available to us to help build up a picture of the Roman way of life.

Make Roman shields and swords and practice military manoeuvres in the school hall.

SMALL GROUP ACTIVITIES

Create a newspaper or magazine of interest to the Romans living in Britain.

Design and make a Roman suit of armour.

Make a model of a Roman room which demonstrates how the hypocaust works (central heating).

Make a model section of Roman road using appropriate materials.

Make a section of Hadrian's Wall which joins with others to make a whole class model.

Construct a large plan of a typical Roman town.

Make mosaic patterns from squares of sticky paper.

Make a life size model/collage of a Roman solidier.

Examine artefacts from a museum loan - debate uses and make careful sketches.

STARTING POINTS

Talk about the Roman conquest and occupation of Britain; the arrival and settlement of the Anglo-Saxons; Viking raids and settlements. Then focus on the Romans.

Listen to a class novel set in Roman times e.g. 'The Eagle of the Ninth' by Rosemary Sutcliff or 'Word of Caesar' by Geoffrey Treace.

Visit to local Roman remains or Roman road.

Visit to local museum to look for evidence of Roman presence in the area.

Construction of a model Roman road or of a section of Hadrian's Wall.

Construction of full size Roman Soldier dressed in appropriate armour.

Recommended Reference Books
From Cavemen to Vikings - R.J. Unstead - Pub. by A & C Black.
Living in Roman Times - Usborne First History.
Ancient Rome - Usborne Everyday Life.
Romans activity book - British Museum.
The Romans - Tim Wood - Paperbird (Ladybird).

RESOURCES/EQUIPMENT

Local museum loan of artefacts or replicas.
BBC - Watch - TV Series "The Romans".
I.T. - Arcventure 1 - The Romans - An archaeological expedition into Roman Times - Sherston Software.
Philip Green A4 picture pack - Romans.
P.C.E.T. wallchart - Roman Britain.
Usborne model to construct - Roman Villa.
Usborne model to construct - Make this Roman Fort.

Possible Visits
Local Roman remains such as Hadrian's Wall or the Romans in Bath. A local museum may have some Roman artefacts in their collection.

Possible Visitors
Curator or Education Officer from Museum.
Amateur archaeologist.

Best Time of Year
Any.

nvaders & Settlers: Romans

ART AND DISPLAY

Draw a picture of your kitchen at home today and then one of a Roman kitchen.

Make a 3D model of a Roman meal.

Make a poster advertising events at e.g. the Colosseum - a chariot race etc.

Make a 3D junk model of the type of garden enjoyed by people living in a Roman villa.

Make a clay tile mosaic - cut up in small pieces and reassemble.

Draw and paint your own portrait in Roman dress. (Or dress a member of the class in a toga to sketch.)

Make a drawing or painting of an everyday object today as though it is a mosaic.

Look at Roman style footwear.

Design a coin with your profile on it.

Design an eagle headed banner to be carried by a Roman Legion.

INDIVIDUAL ACTIVITIES

Draw a plan of a Roman amphitheatre and then make a model.

Make rubbings of reproduction Roman coins.

Make clay replicas of Roman pottery.

Make a map of the Roman Empire.

Sew a picture of a Roman Soldier.

Make a scale drawing of a Roman Fort.

Dye sheep wool and experiment with weaving cloth.

Research one aspect of Roman life e.g. food or dress.

Make a model of a Roman galley; a chariot; simple battering ram; stone throwing machine; catapult etc.

Sketch and label the main parts of a Roman Villa.

END PRODUCT

A collage showing action in the amphitheatre.

Make up individual topic booklets containing stories written and information collected.

A large class model of Hadrian's Wall set in appropriate paper mache landscape.

A display of models made.

Wall size time line showing when the Romans invaded Britain.

Plan and carry out a Roman feast. Research types of food, dress etc. - shop for goods. Plan a date and hold a feast.

Display mosaic patterns made.

Act out a play in which the Roman army takes a leading role. Examples could include the Christmas or Easter stories.

PROGRAMME OF STUDY

Pupils should be taught:
- that there are life processes, including growth, nutrition and reproduction, common to plants
- that plant growth is affected by the availability of light and water, and by temperature
- that plants need light to produce food for growth, and the importance of the leaf in this process
- that the root anchors the plant, and that water and nutrients are taken in through the root and transported through the stem to other parts of the plant
- about the life cycle of flowering plants, including pollination, seed production, seed dispersal and germination
- how locally occurring animals and plants can be identified and assigned to groups, using keys
- that different plants and animals are found in different habitats
- how animals and plants in different habitats are suited to their environment.

SKILLS TO BE DEVELOPED

- to ask questions e.g. How; Why; What will happen if?
- to know how to use first hand experience and simple secondary sources to obtain information
- to be able to relate understanding of science to domestic and environmental contexts
- to consider ways in which science is related to personal health
- to learn how to treat living things and the environment with care and sensitivity
- to relate simple scientific ideas to the evidence for them
- to use scientific vocabulary to name and describe living things, materials, phenomena and processes
- to present scientific information in a number of ways e.g. through drawings, diagrams, tables and charts, and in speech and writing
- to recognise hazards and risks when working with living things and materials
- to follow simple instructions to control the risks to themselves.

SUPPORTING CURRICULUM LINKS

English	-	Write a year in the life of a tree or a woodland creature. Debate the cutting down of woodland areas for housing development.
Maths	-	Estimate the number of leaves on one tree.
Technology	-	Design and build a machine to weigh an insect. Make jam from fruit collected in a wood.
History	-	Examine old O.S. maps to see how local woodlands have diminished over the last 100 years.
Geography	-	Research woodlands found in Tropical Climates. Research how man uses insects e.g. bees, silkworms etc.

WHOLE CLASS ACTIVITIES

Discuss the concept of a "habitat" and name the common life forms that may be found in the habitat to be studied.

Study the major organs and organ systems of flowering plants. Name all the parts of the plant.

Discuss life cycles in plants and animals.

Discuss photosynthesis.

Plan and collect together equipment needed for the exploration of a small woodland habitat. Visit a local habitat and carry out planned investigations. Return to classroom with appropriate samples, notes and sketches. Set up "mini-environments" in the classroom. Return specimens to the original environment after 2 or 3 weeks.

Demonstrate how to use a binocular microscope and binoculars. Demonstrate and practice with class games how to use a simple scientific key.

SMALL GROUP ACTIVITIES

Experiment with growing a variety of seeds, e.g. grow some on a window sill, some in the dark, some in the fridge, some without water etc.

Use magnifiers and a binocular microscope to observe and record life in the various insect houses (the teacher should emphasise the sensitive collection and care of living things).

Use simple scientific keys to identify "minibeasts", different types of trees and woodland birds.

Investigate how snails or worms move.

Investigate what minibeasts eat and the environments they are found in.

Experiment with seed flight or rate of leaf decay.

Use a binocular microscope to examine leaf litter or rotten wood collected from a woodland floor.

STARTING POINTS

A local habitat needs to be visited for this topic e.g. a wood, a park, a hedgerow, stone wall, canal bank, graveyard etc. The topic should be named appropriately.

Visit a local habitat and make sketches and notes. Prepare for a second visit when some samples may be taken. Identify and learn the names of some common plants. Collect samples and then set up a mini environment with small plants and rotten wood; a wormery; a snail house; a woodlouse house; a caterpillar house; etc. Set an insect trap and examine it later.

Recommended Reference Books
The Nature Trail Book of Woodlands - Usborne Books.
Oxford Young Scientist Investigates - Small Garden Animals.

RESOURCES/EQUIPMENT

Simple scientific keys for identifying trees, birds and minibeasts. Binocular microscope, binoculars, specimen holders, plastic tanks, various magnifying glasses.

P.C.E.T. Charts - "Mammals and Their Young" and "Mammals at Night".
I.T. - Badger Trails - Sherston Software Ltd.

Possible Visits
A local wood/park/wasteland.
A nature reserve or country park.
A "wild" part of the school grounds.

Possible Visitors
Country park warden, school groundsman, amateur naturalist etc.

Best Time of Year
Summer term/September for maximum insect life.

In a Wood

ART AND DISPLAY

Create pictures of a wood in different seasons - use this as a basis for colour work e.g. weaving.
Make observational drawings of leaves or give a child half of a leaf and ask them to complete.
Study pictures of woods by different artists e.g. Klint, Mondrian, Bonnard, Van Gogh etc.
Make observational drawings of fruits e.g. sycamore keys, conkers, beech nuts etc. on a large scale.
Take impressions of bark in clay and paint later.
Develop patterns from bark rubbings or make a collage of a piece of bark using yarns, threads, crumpled paper etc.
Look up/down - sketch different views of a wood.
Draw what you see 'framed' in a footshape viewfinder on the ground in the wood.
Draw, paint or make a collage of plants growing under trees.

INDIVIDUAL ACTIVITIES

Make a life cycle dial for a flowering plant and a woodland creature.

Research how birds are equipped with different shaped beaks/claws/wings etc. according to the type of habitat they live in.

Research animals and plants found in a desert habitat.
Research animals and plants found in a watery habitat.

Draw and paint images seen down a microscope.

Make animal models from woodland fruits or clay.

Study in depth a 30cm square of woodland floor.

Make plaster casts of animal footprints found in mud.

Make a giant 3D model insect.

END PRODUCT

A large frieze showing where different insects/animals/plants would be found in and around a woodland habitat.

Individual topic booklets containing written accounts of visits/observations made and research carried out.

A collection of rotten wood, old birds nests, plaster casts of feet marks etc. found during visits made.

Collections of pressed leaves, fruits, bark rubbings, models made etc.

A large picture of a tree showing the names of all the parts.

Display and tasting session of home made jam.

PROGRAMME OF STUDY

Question the use of local buildings. What is a house used for? What makes a house a home? What is a school, post office, shop, cinema, leisure centre etc. used for? Groups of people called Christians have a special building called a church, chapel, cathedral or meeting hall; Muslims a Mosque; Sikhs a Gurdwara; Buddhists a Temple; Jews a Synagogue etc.

Question the uses made of these buildings by individuals, families and the local communities.

Visit several local places of worship and note the main features. Find out what they represent and how the buildings differ. Attempt to find out what worship means to a believer.

SKILLS TO BE DEVELOPED

Study religious beliefs and practices and relate them to one's own experience.

Enter imaginatively into the motivations, feelings, responses, experiences, hopes, aspirations, beliefs, values, attitudes and perceptions of religious believers. (Planning R.E. in Schools C.E.M.)

Think deeply about and question sensitive aspects of human experience.

SUPPORTING CURRICULUM LINKS

English	-	Make a copy in joined handwriting of Hymn or Prayer used in worship. Talk to a believer about their worship. Discuss who/what is worshipped. Write poems/creative writing on the theme "Worship is........" or "During worship........".
Maths	-	Calculate area of floor. Calculate number of stones/bricks used in construction.
Science	-	Look for examples of wildlife in graveyards.
Technology	-	Design methods of lifting stone to build a medieval Cathedral.
History	-	Research how old local places of worship are. Display on a timeline. Study old street maps.
Geography	-	Draw plans of places of worship.
Music	-	Learn a modern Christian hymn or song from another faith.
P.E./Drama	-	Act out simple acts of ritual that are used in some acts of worship e.g. Eucharist.

WHOLE CLASS ACTIVITIES

Plan and carry out a visit to local place of worship. Make plans of the building and grounds. Sketch and note the main features found inside and out.

Devise appropriate questions to interview a leader or member of the religious community.

Carry out an interview with a believer or religious leader.

Visit other places of worship and carry out further interviews. Discuss similarities and differences.

Discuss symbols found in places of worship and their significance.

Interview a religious leader and find out about all the jobs he/she has to carry out. Write "A day in the life of ....".

Discuss how the Bible/Holy Books are used in worship.

Talk about the feelings associated with places of worship visited.

Listen to and discuss different types of music used during worship.

SMALL GROUP ACTIVITIES

Collect rubbings and information from graveyard headstones. Make sketches.

List the differences/similarities found in different places of Christian worship.

Match religious symbols with appropriate faiths and places of worship.

Study documents e.g. Baptismal Records.

Research outreach work carried out locally by believers and work overseas.

Research and sketch different types of architecture found in Churches. Make your own designs using repeating patterns observed.

Study examples, discuss and write a group prayer which could be used in an act of worship.

STARTING POINTS

Discuss/debate/reflect what a church/chapel/mosque may be used for.

Make a visit to a local place of worship. Study external and internal physical features of note. Discuss with religious leader or member of the community what the physical features represent.

Talk to a believer about worship.

Participate in a quiet time of reflection inside the building.

Books
What to look for inside a Church - Ladybird
What to look for outisde a Church - Ladybird
Religious Buildings - J. Mayled - Wayland
Exploring a theme - Places of Worship - C.E.M.

RESOURCES/EQUIPMENT

Dictionary; Encyclopedia; School Library; Slides; Videos etc.

A good collection of children's reference books which touch on the theme.

Posters which show places of worship e.g. Places of Worship by Pictorial Educational Trust. Examples of artifacts used in worship.

Possible Visits
Several local Christian places of worship e.g. Anglican Church, Catholic Church, Methodist Church, a Cathedral etc.
A place of worship belonging to another major world faith e.g. a Mosque.

Possible Visitors
A religious leader e.g. Priest, Vicar, Minister, Rabbi etc.
A typical believer from a religious community. A worker from a faith that helps care for the building.

Best Time of Year
Any

Places of Worship

ART AND DISPLAY

Collect pictures of places of worship from around the world e.g. temples, mosques, churches etc. and use as a basis for pattern work. Incorporate shapes of doorways, windows, roof tops, domes etc.

Make patterns/collage based on stained glass windows, mosaics on walls and floors etc.

Design a prayer mat/kneeler/banner/shawl/head covering for a particular place of worship.

Examine artefacts e.g. candlesticks, incense burners, bells or religious symbols. Draw a composition using several symbols of a particular religion.

Make observational drawings of places of worship both inside and out in your locality. Focus on particular views e.g. through a doorway, partial views etc.

INDIVIDUAL ACTIVITIES

Sketch/research types of buildings used in worship by various faiths.

Make detailed sketch and description of a piece of church furniture e.g. font.

Draw a detailed plan showing use of rooms in a place of worship.

Research the activities which take place during a baptism or marriage service.

Recreate a banner or kneeler design found in a church.

Make cardboard models of places of worship.

Design and make stained glass windows.

Write a personal account of a wedding or baptism you have attended.

END PRODUCT

Display of written and creative work or individual booklets made.

Make a collection of old Bibles, certificates of Baptism or other personal artifacts connected with worship.

Make a display of plans made at different places of worship.

Make a large accurate whole class model of a local church.

Make a class frieze which depicts scenes from a wedding ceremony.

Make a gallery of sketches made "on location" in places of worship.

Lead a whole school act of worship including some aspects of worship observed locally.

PROGRAMME OF STUDY

Pupils should be taught:
- to design and make simple products
- carry out practical tasks in which they develop and practice particular skills and knowledge (in this case - how simple mechanisms can be used to produce different types of movement)
- take part in activities in which they investigate, disassemble and evaluate simple products
- work with a range of materials and components
- work independently and in teams
- apply skills, knowledge and understanding from other subjects e.g. The following is from the science programme of study
- to compare everyday materials e.g. paper, polythene etc. on the basis of their properties, including strength and flexibility, and to relate these properties to everyday uses of materials.

SKILLS TO BE DEVELOPED

Designing Skills
- generate ideas
- clarify ideas and suggest ways forward
- consider appearance, function, safety and reliability
- model ideas to explore aspects of the design
- evaluate design ideas and look for improvements
- develop a clear idea of what has to be done
Making Skills
- select appropriate materials, tools and techniques
- measure, mark out, cut and shape a range of materials using appropriate tools and equipment
- join and combine materials and components accurately in temporary and permanent ways
- apply finishing techniques appropriate to the purpose of the product
- evaluate the product by carrying out appropriate tests
- implement improvements identified as being necessary

SUPPORTING CURRICULUM LINKS

English	-	Write simple plays to be performed. Read books to find simple stories to animate.
Maths	-	Measure puppet shapes. Draw larger/smaller scale drawings.
Science	-	Compare materials to discover strengths, flexibility, ability to be coloured, joined cut etc.
Geography	-	Research Javanese stick puppets.
History	-	Research Puppets from different cultures past and present.
Music	-	Movement - 'Coppelia'.
R.E.	-	Explore emotions/problems with bullying etc.

WHOLE CLASS ACTIVITIES

Colour materials to form background colour on large piece of material approx. 42cm x 42cm. The best material to use is old white cotton sheets collected by the children.

Techniques for colouring could include: direct application of colour, e.g. felt tips, wax crayons applied to paper and ironed on to material, pastels, paints, stencilling, rolling, printing, splashing etc. resist dying - tie and dye, marbelling, dip and dye, batik etc.

Look at examples and then experiment with stick puppets and marionettes.

Teach sewing techniques e.g. running, stitch, blanket stitch, sewing on buttons, attaching hair by looping and cutting.

SMALL GROUP ACTIVITIES

Decide which of the moving puppets they are going to create in permanent ways in groups.

Discuss ways in which the model may be constructed.

Individually draw designs.

Debate with an adult and the rest of the group the best design points to be used.

Finalise the design.

Allocate tasks and collect appropriate materials.

Build the moving puppets.

Test the puppets and look for improvements.

Build improvements into puppets.

STARTING POINTS

Talk about/demonstrate different types of puppets. Watch a puppet video e.g. Muppets, early B.B.C., Button Moon etc.

Teach how joints can be made to create puppet movement e.g. meccano nuts and bolts; drilling strip wood and joining with string, pipe cleaners, paper fasteners etc; drilling dowel/strip wood and join with screw eyes; dowel and material glued and stapled, felt tip pen barrels threaded with string with a wooden bead at the joint, paper clips bound with tape linked together.

Recap/teach techniques for cutting, joining and colouring hard and soft materials.

Teach pupils that anything that will colour paper will colour fabric in a non permanent way.

Recommended Reference Books
The Know How Book of Puppets - Usbourne.
Technology from Puppets - Gary Morris - T.T.S.

RESOURCES/EQUIPMENT

Different types of puppets e.g. glove, stick, rod, shadow, marionettes.

A variety of materials e.g. plastic tubing, strip wood, fabrics, card, socks, polyspheres, plastic cups, paper plates, spoons, fabric cotton and polycotton.

Colouring materials may include: wax crayons, pencils, felt pens, paints, inks etc.

A selection of appropriate tools for cutting and drilling.

P.C.E.T. wallchart "Puppets".

Possible Visits
Toy collections in local museums.

Possible Visitors
Local Theatre group to give demonstration of use of puppets.

Best Time of Year
Any.

Design and Make: Puppets from Textiles
(materials)

ART AND DISPLAY

Make a display of different types of puppets including word lists/materials/how made etc.

Display books with puppets as a character e.g. Pinochio or puppets from other parts of the world e.g. shadow puppets.

Collect pictures of T.V. puppets e.g. Thunderbirds, Sooty, Muppets, Punch and Judy etc.

Display "try out designs" from sketch books.

Display examples of different techniques for making moving joints.

Display different techniques/materials for making puppet heads.

INDIVIDUAL ACTIVITIES

Choose background material - not neccesarily one's own or select material with an existing colour/simple pattern.

Decide on type/character of puppet to be made. Design and collect ideas in sketchbook as an animated drawing.

Seek help and suggestions from others.

Design and make own glove/rod/string/paper bag/paper plate/plastic spoon puppets.

Make observational drawings of puppets brought in by children.

END PRODUCT

Individually or in small groups perform a simple play/tell a story using the puppets made.

Invite infant children/parents/older members of the community to watch.

Take puppet show "on tour" to local church, residential home or neighbouring school.

Tell a story for assembly using puppets.

A display of all puppets completed with sketches showing processes gone through.

PROGRAMME OF STUDY

A contrasting locality in the United Kingdom should be studied. This should be similar in size to the locality of the school.

Pupils should be taught:
- about the main physical and human features
- how this locality may be similar and how it may differ from home
- how the features of a locality influence the nature and location of human activities within it
- about recent and proposed changes in the locality
- how the locality is set within a broader geographical context and linked with other places

In investigating how environments change, pupils should be taught:
- how people affect the environment, e.g. *by quarrying; building reservoirs; building motorways*
- how and why people seek to manage and sustain their environment, e.g. *by combatting river pollution, by organic farming, conserving areas of beautiful landscape or of scientific value*

SKILLS TO BE DEVELOPED

- observe and question about geographical features and issues, collect/record evidence to answer questions, analyse, draw conclusions and communicate findings
- use appropriate geographical vocabulary to describe and interpret their surroundings
- undertake fieldwork using appropriate instruments
- make maps and plans at a variety of scales
- use and interpret globes, and maps and plans at a variety of scales; the work should include using co-ordinates and four-figure grid references, measuring direction and distance, following routes, using the contents page and index of an atlas, and identifying the points of reference specified on the Geog. N.C. maps
- use secondary sources of evidence to provide information e.g. pictures; photographs (including aerial photographs) T.V.; radio; books; newspapers; visitors
- use IT to gain access to additional information sources and to assist in handling, classifying and presenting evidence.

SUPPORTING CURRICULUM LINKS

English	-	Write a description of your ideal holiday destination. Write poems about work/industry.
Maths	-	Use the scale on maps to calculate distances between major towns.
Science	-	Research how T.V. communications are sent from region to region.
Technology	-	Design a set of clothes to cope with the extremes of U.K. weather conditions.
History	-	Talk about the history of the Union Jack.
Music	-	Listen to, learn and comment on traditional English/Welsh/Scottish/Northern Irish music.
P.E.	-	Role play the movement of a parcel from one end of the country to the other.

WHOLE CLASS ACTIVITIES

Talk at length about the pupils experiences of visiting different parts of the U.K.

Make maps of the U.K. based on Map A in the National Curriculum. Make maps which show physical features, main towns and cities, routes of communication, etc. Make maps which show the counties of the U.K.

List the features (physical and human) that make your locality unique.

Use the information collected on the 'Contrasting Locality Visit' to construct an A3/A4 fact sheet.

Discuss the similarities and differences between the two localities.

Carry out a survey of jobs done by parents. Talk about natural resources and man-made products. Discuss how work may be linked to regional resources and industries.

Talk about the places in the U.K. children have been on holiday, likes and dislikes, and main physical features.

SMALL GROUP ACTIVITIES

Using information collected, make up an A3/A4 fact sheet which informs about car making in Sunderland or Birmingham; the oil industry in Aberdeen; steel making in Sheffield; the chemical industry in Teeside; pottery making in Staffordshire; farming in Lincolnshire; fishing from Hull and Grimsby etc.

Using information collected, make up your own holiday brochure for Blackpool, the Lake District, the Scottish Isles etc. List the reasons people like to go to these places on holiday.

Cost a journey for a family of four from your locality to your chosen holiday resort. Compare cost of transport by coach, car, train, aeroplane. Give reasons for your preferred mode of transport.

Use co-ordinates to locate places on a U.K. map.

Devise your own business enterprise and carry it out.

STARTING POINTS

Illustrate or debate main physical features of home locality. Discuss man made features. Decide if your locality is urban or rural; sea-side or inland etc.

Use maps to search for a contrasting locality within about twenty miles. Plan/carry out a day visit and use this to collect as much evidence as possible about the locality e.g. photographs, leaflets, sketches, interviews, notes etc. Visit the local school.

Write to a number of large industries up and down the country requesting information on their products.

Write to a number of holiday resorts up and down the country requesting information about their attractions.

Recommended Reference Books
Britain - Maps and Mapwork - Macmillan Education.
Looking at Britain - Gadsby - A & C Black.
We Live in Britain - C. Fairclough - Wayland.
Book of Britain - Williamson & Meredith - Usborne.
Welsh for Beginners - Language Guides - Usborne.

RESOURCES/EQUIPMENT

U.K. wall maps.
A class set of Atlases.
Holiday postcards and brochures.
I.T. - 'Britain by Rail' and 'Catch' computer simulations available from AVP.
PCET wallcharts - wood, wool and making a mug - three packs of charts.

Possible Visits
A visit to a local factory or farm, bus station, railway station, motorway service station or a parcel sorting office.

Possible Visitors
A visitor from another part of the U.K.
A train driver, lorry driver, airline pilot to talk about their work.

Best Time of Year
Any

Localities in the U.K.

ART AND DISPLAY

Collect holiday brochures for the U.K. Using cut out pictures design a poster to advertise one locality.

Display a collection of guide books, photographs, postcards etc. from different localities.

Look at flags, national symbols, stamps, money etc. from different parts of the U.K. Design a new version of each based on these or use originals for observational drawing.

Collect traditional items from different parts of the U.K. e.g. dolls in national dress. Draw or make similar models or design new versions.

Design a logo to represent Scotland incorporating as many distinctive features as possible.

Make a plan of your 'ideal' village or sea-side resort.

Make a frieze of a busy motorway, railway station or airport.

INDIVIDUAL ACTIVITIES

Write a letter to a "pen-pal" in a school in a contrasting locality.

Glue a holiday postcard in the centre of an A4 page. List all the physical features and man-made features you can see.

Examine household objects e.g. vacuum cleaner, bar of chocolate etc. for items made in the U.K. Draw a map which shows where the product was made.

Devise a "British Isles" quiz.

Research and build a model farm/fishing boat etc.

Make a plan of a railway terminal/airport which shows how goods are loaded and unloaded.

Paint pictures of national flags.

Design a poster to sell goods from a factory you have visited or know about.

Design a poster to advertise your chosen U.K. holiday destination.

END PRODUCT

Hold a great debate: having established the need to work and that different industries exist and most people like to go to scenic places such as the countryside/sea-side to holiday debate:

A proposed new factory next to a pleasant housing estate.

A proposed new motorway through an area of outstanding natural beauty.

A proposed new shopping and leisure development on the site of a nature reserve at the edge of town.

A proposed open-cast mine in a National Park.

Compile individual topic booklets containing stories written and information collected.

Share A4 fact sheets with others in class.

PROGRAMME OF STUDY

Pupils should be taught:
- that a complete circuit, including a battery or power supply, is needed to make electrical devices work
- how switches can be used to control electrical devices
- ways of varying the current in a circuit to make bulbs brighter or dimmer
- how to represent series circuits by drawings and diagrams, and how to construct series circuits on the basis of drawings and diagrams.
- that some materials are better electrical conductors than others
- that there are forces of attraction and repulsion between magnets, and forces of attraction between magnets and magnetic materials

(From Design and Technology, Programme of Study):
Pupils should be taught:
- how electrical circuits, including those with simple switches, can be used to achieve functional results

SKILLS TO BE DEVELOPED

- to be able to turn ideas suggested to them, and their own ideas, into a form that can be investigated
- to know that making predictions can be useful when planning what to do
- to decide what evidence should be collected
- to know that changing one factor and observing and measuring the effect, whilst keeping other factors the same, allows a fair test or comparison to be made
- to consider what apparatus and equipment to use
- to use simple apparatus and equipment correctly
- to make careful observations and measurements
- to check observations and measurements by repeating them
- to use tables, bar charts and line graphs to present results
- to make comparisons and to identify trends or patterns in results
- to use results to draw conclusions
- to indicate whether the evidence collected supports any prediction made
- to try to explain conclusions in terms of scientific knowledge and understanding

SUPPORTING CURRICULUM LINKS

English - Write about "The Day the Electricity ran out." Debate: "Would you be prepared to use less electrical devices (e.g. no T.V. or computer games) to save the planet's energy resources?

Maths - Solve problems involving the cost of electricity

History - Research the work of Michael Faraday. Interview local people about their first experiences of electricity

Geography - Research hydro-electric power. Research other fuels used to generate electricity including solar power and wind power.

Technology - Make up a detailed design drawing showing how electricity from a power station may supply a small town.

WHOLE CLASS ACTIVITIES

Discuss dangers of "Mains Electricity". Watch a safety video available from The Electricity Council.

Design and paint warning posters.

Demonstrate how simple circuits can be made safely using torch batteries (not car batteries!!) Warn about dangerous chemicals in all batteries.

Demonstrate the properties of various types of magnets. Talk about the forces involved and how these can be represented in diagrams.

Make up own symbols for bulbs, switches and other electrical components. Introduce children to common symbols used.

Talk about series and parallel circuits.

SMALL GROUP ACTIVITIES

Experiment with:

How to light one/two/three bulbs.
How to add a switch to a circuit.
How to vary the current in a circuit.
How to construct circuits from simple drawings.
How to test for conductors and insulators.
How strong bar magnets are.
How strong horse-shoe magnets are.
Which is the most attractive part of a magnet.

STARTING POINTS

Make a collection of toys powered by batteries.
Talk about what the batteries make the toys do.
Visit a power station to find out just how electricity is made.
Talk about the dangers of mains electricity in the home.
Devise/hold a Home Safety Quiz.
Listen to a guest speaker talk about his/her work.

Recommended Reference Books
Oxford Young Scientist Investigates - "Electricity and Magnetism."

"Science with Batteries" - Usborne Books.

Electricity and Magnestism Photocopiable Activities - Topical Resources.

Understanding Electricity - a catalogue of resources available from The Electricity Council.

RESOURCES/EQUIPMENT

Batteries, wires, bulbs and holders, small electric motors, buzzers, bells, switches, crocodile clips etc.

P.C.E.T. Wallcharts "Conserving Energy" and "Global Energy".

I.T. - Simple Circuits - a program which simulates simple circuits - Electricity Council.

Possible Visits
A power station.

Possible Visitors
A public relations officer from an electricity company. An electrician to demonstrate tools and talk about his work.

Best Time of Year
Any.

Electricity & Magnetism

ART AND DISPLAY

Display/use for observational drawing objects that need electricity to make them work.

Design a poster to warn of the dangers of electricity.

Draw an electric plug from different view points. Look at the different designs available for an electrical gadget e.g. a kettle - incorporate several of the shapes to make a border.

Draw instructions as to how to programme a video - wire a plug - make a cup of tea.

Look at the logos of the different electricity boards - design a new one for your locality.

Make a collection of fridge magnets - design a range of new ones based on e.g. storybook characters.

Make patterns in iron filings - draw what happens - develop in black and white and then into a coloured composition based on the shapes that have emerged.

INDIVIDUAL ACTIVITIES

Design and build a model which contains a simple electric circuit. Examples could include: a model lighthouse, a model car with headlamps or indicators, a dolls house, a power station with working pylons, a puppet theatre, a robot, a quiz board to answer questions at the touch of a button, a burglar alarm etc.

Design and build a game for two which uses magnets.

Make a chart which shows all the different uses for electricity in the home.

Research some of the attempts to build electric cars. What are the advantages and disadvantages of these vehicles?

END PRODUCT

Hold an exhibition of models built by the children which contain simple circuits. Invite in parents, infant children, other classes etc. for guided tours of the exhibition.

Make up individual topic booklets containing reports from experiments, information collected, stories etc.

Make a display or collection of old pieces of electrical equipment.

Race models powered by electric motors.

PROGRAMME OF STUDY

Pupils should be taught about some of the major events and personalities, including monarchs, and the way of life of people at different levels of society in Tudor times:

- Henry VIII and the break with Rome, e.g. *the divorce question, the dissolution of the monasteries*
- exploration overseas, e.g. *the voyages of Sebastian and John Cabot, Francis Drake and Walter Raleigh*
- Elizabeth I and the Armada (1588)
- Court life, e.g. *the progresses of Elizabeth I, the role of a personality such as Thomas More or the Earl of Essex*
- ways of life in town and country, e.g. *home life, work and leisure, health, trade*
- arts and architecture, including Shakespeare, e.g. *Elizabethan theatres, music, paintings, town houses, manor houses, and country houses and their estates.*

SKILLS TO BE DEVELOPED

- to be able to place events, people and changes in periods studied within a chronological framework
- to be able to use dates and terms relating to the passing of time, including ancient, modern, BC, AD, century and decade
- to have an understanding of the characteristic features of particular periods and societies
- to be able to describe and identify reasons for and the results of main events and changes in the periods studied and make links across periods
- to be able to identify and give reasons for different ways in which the past is represented and interpreted
- to be able to find out about aspects of the periods studied from a range of sources of information including documents and printed sources, artefacts, pictures and photographs, music and buildings and sites
- to know the terms necessary to describe the periods and topics studied, including court, monarch, parliament, nation, civilisations, invasion, conquest, settlement, conversion, slavery, trade, industry, law.

SUPPORTING CURRICULUM LINKS

English	-	Write "My Voyage on the Golden Hind". Debate "Our World - Flat or Round?", "The rights and wrongs of this new trade in people." Read a short extract from William Shakespeare.
Maths	-	Calculate the stores required to feed a ships crew for a fixed period of time.
Science	-	Experiment with getting tall sailing ships to stay upright in water. Investigate the problems of carrying cannon.
Technology	-	Design and make a bed with a rope matress large enough for a doll. Make appropriate bed clothes for it.
Geography	-	Discuss the problems caused to country people by the enclosure of land.
Music	-	Attempt to sing Elizabethan madrigals. Listen and respond to music from Tudor England.
R.E.	-	Examine copies of King Jame's Bible. Talk about how it came to be written.

WHOLE CLASS ACTIVITIES

Make a time line which shows where Tudor times fit into British history.

Make a time line which shows the Tudor Kings and Queens.

Talk about Henry VIII and his six wives, and the creation of the Church of England.

Dramatise life on a long sea voyage of exploration.

Map routes taken by famous explorers such as Drake or Raleigh.

Make a map of the known world before voyages of discovery.

Learn about life around the court of Henry VIII and Elizabeth I.

Investigate the story of the Armada from the Spanish and the English point of view.

Discuss what evidence is available to help us build up a picture of the Tudor way of life e.g. Shakespeare plays, the letters of Henry VIII, local government records, surviving buildings, Tudor archeological sites such as the Mary Rose, inventories of possessions etc.

SMALL GROUP ACTIVITIES

Compile an information sheet about each of the Tudor monarchs.

Map the route of the Spanish Armada and mark positions of wrecked ships.

Research the building of the first theatre. Make up a short play and act it out.

Design a game in which sailing ships engage in battle around the coast of Britain.

Plan the equipment needed for a group of people to colonise a new country.

Make a ship's log for a voyage of discovery.

Carry out the Mary Rose computer simulation.

Devise a document written with a quill and signed with a seal.

Make a strip cartoon telling of the dissolution of a monastery.

STARTING POINTS

Construct a large whole class model of a Tudor Fighting Ship.
Through drama, explore some of the different tasks involved in sailing and living in a Tudor ship.
Visit a Tudor Mansion.
Visit the site of a ruined abbey and imagine the day it was torn down.
Listen to a class novel set in Tudor Times e.g. When Beacons Blazed - Hester Burton; The Queen Elizabeth Story - Rosemary Sutcliff.
Read pupil novels such as The King's Ship; The Women in Black; Master Will's New Theatre - Pub. by Anglia Young Books.

Recommended Reference Books
Tudors and Stuarts - R.J. Unstead - Published by A & C Black.
The Tudors - T. Wood - Paperbird (Ladybird).
The Spanish Armada - Ladybird.

RESOURCES/EQUIPMENT

Tudor Life Support Materials - Anglia Young Books.
History Quick Reads - Stories of Tudor Times - Pub. by Anglia Young Books.
Postcards of Tudor portraits available from the National Portrait Gallery.
Cassette of Tudor England music - available from Longman Primary Music, Longman House, Harlow.
I.T. - Mary Rose - The Anatomy of a Tudor Warship - Cambridge Software House.

Possible Visits
Remains of a monastery.
A Tudor building.
A local museum/antiques shop to examine Tudor artefacts.
A local church with Tudor architecture.

Possible Visitors
The curator/education officer of a local museum.
A local historian or antiques dealer.

Best Time of Year
Any

Life in Tudor Times

ART AND DISPLAY

Look at Holbein portraits - paint your friend in Tudor costume in the style of Holbein.

Look at black and white pattern on Tudor houses - using cut paper strips. Develop a black and white pattern based on these.

Look at miniatures - paint a face real or imaginary as though it is a miniature.

Look at knot gardens designs using pictures from magazines. Design a knot garden of your own.

Using a range of collage material create a textured portrait of Elizabeth I - look at paintings by Hilliard.

Make a Tudor hat or headress.

Make a four poster bed - Tudor House - Market Place.

Design a menu for an Elizabethan banquet.

Design a wall hanging/tapestry for a house - that tells a story/depicts an Elizabethan event.

INDIVIDUAL ACTIVITIES

Draw an illustrated family tree for Henry VIII.

Research one aspect of Tudor life e.g. punishments, food, sports, pastimes, dress etc.

Make a model Tudor ship.

Make a model Tudor house with wooden frames and chimney. Combine with others to make a street scene.

Make a wattle and daub section of wall.

Make small clay bricks and with others build a model brick house. List advantages and disadvantages of two types of construction.

Use local records to find out about everyday life in the towns.

Draw a cross-section of a Tudor warship.

Sketch pictures of early fire arms.

Make collage figures for a Tudor scene.

END PRODUCT

Act out a court scene and hand out Tudor style punishments for various crimes.

Make up individual topic booklets containing stories written and information collected.

Make a large model of the Armada sea battle.

Make a model street scene with houses, horses, carts, market stalls etc.

Make a frieze of a Tudor street scene.

Hold a competition to see who has devised the most interesting/exciting "Sea Battle Game".

Act out a small part of a play by William Shakespeare in Elizabethan dress.

PROGRAMME OF STUDY

Pupils should be taught:
- that there are life processes, including nutrition, movement, growth and reproduction, common to animals, including humans
- the functions of teeth and the importance of dental care
- that food is needed for activity and for growth, and that an adequate and varied diet is needed to keep healthy
- a simple model of the structure of the heart and how it acts as a pump
- how blood circulates in the body through arteries and veins
- the effect of exercise and rest on pulse rate
- that humans have skeletons and muscles to support their bodies and to help them to move
- the main stages of the human life cycle
- that tobacco, alcohol and other drugs can have harmful effects.

SKILLS TO BE DEVELOPED

- to ask questions e.g. How; Why; What will happen if?
- to know how to use first hand experience and simple secondary sources to obtain information
- to be able to relate understanding of science to domestic and environmental contexts
- to consider ways in which science is related to personal health
- to learn how to treat living things and the environment with care and sensitivity
- to relate simple scientific ideas to the evidence for them
- to use scientific vocabulary to name and describe living things, materials, phenomena and processes
- to present scientific information in a number of ways e.g. through drawings, diagrams, tables and charts, and in speech and writing
- to recognise hazards and risks when working with living things and materials
- to follow simple instructions to control the risks to themselves.

SUPPORTING CURRICULUM LINKS

English	-	Listen to "The Borrowers" or "The Shrinking of Tree Horn" by P. Heide and write "The day I shrank to the size of........."
Maths	-	Make a graph of favourite foods.
Technology	-	Design and make a model stethoscope. Design and make annotated drawings of a safe children's playground.
Science	-	Research the life processes of a mammal.
History	-	Research the work of surgeons before anaesthetics were invented. Listen to Roahl Dahl's visits to the doctor in "Boy".
Geography	-	Collect pictures of people who suffer from poor diets and design a poster requesting aid.
P.E.	-	Carry out a keep fit routine at least three times a week.
R.E.	-	Explore "good" and "bad" feelings in personal relationships.

WHOLE CLASS ACTIVITIES

Talk about the main organs inside the body and the jobs they do.

Talk about the structure of the body and the role of the skeleton and the muscles.

Make diagrams/models of the heart and talk about the flow of blood around the body.

Discuss the importance of healthy eating and the contents of balanced meals.

Talk about the importance of keeping clean and the spread of disease.

Experiment with an old tooth left for some time in a "cola type" drink.

Chart the physical changes in a human life span.

In line with the School Sex Education Policy teach about reproduction.

Demonstrate a cigarette being inhaled by a plastic bottle containing cotton wool. Discuss the harmful effects of alcohol and drugs.

SMALL GROUP ACTIVITIES

Investigate:
How many times you breath in one minute after walking, running or resting.
The best materials for warm clothes.
The best materials to dry ourselves with.
Teeth and disclosing tablets.
How long you can hold a heavy weight in the air.
The volume of air inside your lungs.
The force exerted by a leg.
How hard you can push.
How hard you can pull.
How strong is your finger.
How strong is your grip.
How quick are your reactions.
How good are your eyes.
How well you can hear.

STARTING POINTS

Make full size or individual "A4" size 3D diagrams/models of the human body with "flaps" to lift up to disclose the main organs e.g. brain, heart, lungs, stomach, intestines, kidneys etc.

Talk about keeping fit and the importance of stamina, strength and suppleness. Devise a simple set of exercises to encourage fitness and carry them out at least three times a week for the period of the topic. Measure individual ability to high jump, long jump, run 50m, throw a ball etc. before and after.

Recommended Reference Books
The Young Scientist Investigates - The Human Body - Oxford.
What's Inside You? - Usborne Books.
The Pop-Up Body Book - Jonathon Miller - Pub. by Jonathon Cape Ltd and David Pelham.

RESOURCES/EQUIPMENT

Bathroom scales; height measure; eye-test chart etc.

The Human Body 3D Charts - NES Arnold.
Philip Green Picture Pack - The Human Body.
I.T. - Bodymapper - Pub. by ed IT or The Ultimate Human Body - Pub. Dorling Kindersley.

Possible Visits
Local clinic - dentist - optician - Doctor's surgery etc.

Possible Visitors
School doctor, nurse, dentist, home safety officer, etc.

A volunteer mother to bath a baby.

Best Time of Year
Summer/early Autumn to exercise outside.

The Body Machine

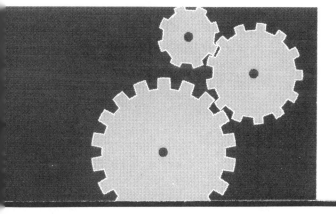

ART AND DISPLAY

Draw a design based on photographs of cells/the blood etc. as seen through a microscope.

Make a collection of different eyes/noses/ears/mouths from pupils in your class.

Draw a series of pictures to show change from babyhood to old age.

Draw ideas for how you might improve/alter change the body machine.

What illnesses has your body machine suffered - or repairs have been done to it? - Illustrate.

Collect pictures of people who help us look after our body machine - design a badge for each one to show what they do.

Look at the ways/clothing etc. we need to protect our body machine - draw - add new designs that might be necessary in the future.

INDIVIDUAL ACTIVITIES

Examine food labels for a typical meal to establish the balance of proteins, carbohydrates and fats.

Research how an eye works.

Research how an ear works.

Make a book of "My body measurements" and enter into class data base. Interrogate when finished for tallest, shortest, largest feet in class etc.

Make a moving model arm joint.

Make a chart showing work of vitamins and foods that provide them.

Take your own fingerprints and compare with others.

Name different muscles on a muscle chart.

Collect newspaper cuttings which report the use of drugs in sport.

END PRODUCT

Full size display of human body with flaps to lift to find the rib cage, heart, lungs etc.

Individual booklets containing reports from experiments, information collected, stories written etc.

Make measurements of individual ability in high jump, long jump etc. at the end of the study to see if individual performance have improved.

Devise and carry out a home safety quiz.

Make a display of posters requesting charity aid or posters promoting Healthy Eating, Drinking and Driving, Taking Exercise, The Dangers of Smoking etc.

PROGRAMME OF STUDY

Question the meaning of "something special". What is special to me? How would you look after a special or favourite book? Groups of people called Christians have a special book called the Bible; Muslims the Quran; Sikhs the Guru Granth Sahib etc. Study examples and stories and teachings from some special books. Find out what these 'special books' mean to believers, how they are used in worship etc.

Investigate the history of writing and printing over a long period of time - from the earliest written forms to modern printing. Find out how stories were passed on before the written form.

SKILLS TO BE DEVELOPED

Study beliefs and practices and relate them to one's own experience.

Enter imaginatively into the motivations, feelings, responses, experiences, hopes, aspirations, beliefs, values, attitudes and perceptions of religious believers. (Planning R.E. in Schools - C.E.M.)

Think deeply about and question sensitive aspects of human experience.

SUPPORTING CURRICULUM LINKS

English - Look at examples of Greek and Hebrew. Look at Bibles translated into languages other than your own. Listen to the story of Mary Jones and her quest for a Bible of her own and discuss. Listen to stories from a number of different religious traditions - discuss their meaning.

Maths - Estimate Goliath's height and compare with Biblical accounts.

Science - Experiment with different printing inks and mixes.

Technology - Design and make a simple printing machine.

History - Research Caxton and his printing press.

Geography - Make a map of the Bible lands.

Drama - Role play a ritual connected with a sacred book.

WHOLE CLASS ACTIVITIES

Make a collection of favourite books. Talk about the choices individuals have made. Share why they are special. Make a collection/display of different Bibles. Talk about how the Bible is made up and what the different parts represent.

Create a book 'special' to your class where every member makes a contribution. Plan what it is to look like. Reproduce for each member to own a copy plus classroom copy. Bind with decorated covers. Discuss where class copy is to be kept.

Study pictures/examples of other religious books. Interview people who see them as special. Ask the question why?

Discuss the history of writing and printing - how we know events took place long ago through: story telling - cave/tomb etchings - clay tablets - scrolls - hand written books - printing etc.

Write/reflect on the theme "What makes a book special".

SMALL GROUP ACTIVITIES

Create a simple illustrated story book to tell an O.T. story to a younger child.

Create a comic strip story version of a N.T. story.

Compare the text of a children's Bible with the same story in various adult Bibles.

Read a parable Jesus told and write about what it could mean. Compare your ideas with others.

Invent a Bible Quiz/Bible Board Game with answers to be found in a children's Bible.

Make recycled paper.

Study one or two stories from religious books in detail e.g. Noah's Ark.

STARTING POINTS

Discuss the meaning of "Special".
Make a collection of our special things.
Make a collection of our special books.
Ask a Christian/other faith believer to talk about their special book.
Make a collection of different types of Bible/special books and study differences between them.
Play Chinese Whispers. Listen to a story told rather than read. Discuss how a story may change with many tellings.
Debate "Why the Bible is special to Christians".

Recommended Reference Books

How Our Bible Came to us - Meryl Doney - Lion Books. The Lion (hardback) or The Puffin (paperback).
Children's Bible - retold by Pat Alexander.
Exploring a theme "Special Books" - C.E.M.

RESOURCES/EQUIPMENT

Dictionary; Encyclopedia; School Library; Slides; Videos; etc.
P.C.E.T. wallcharts - "The Story of the Bible", "Holy Writings".
A good collection of children's reference books which touch on the theme.
Polystyrene sheets and printing inks. Quill pens and black ink.

Possible Visits

Visits to various places of worship to see how the 'special book' is kept/reguarded. Visit a printers/newspaper to see the printing process in action.

Possible Visitors

A leader/follower of a faith to talk about their special book. A printer/newspaper reporter to talk about the printing process.

Best Time of Year
Any

Special Books

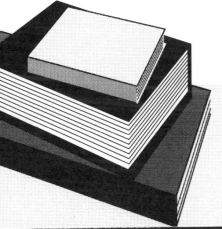

ART AND DISPLAY

Display a collection of special books e.g. autograph books, books containing collections, baby books, scrap books, photo albums (present style and Victorian style).

Design a cover that could be used for a special book of your own.

Look at books that are designed for a baby, an old person, a blind person etc. Discuss in what way they are special to/for them and then design a page that could be included in one of them.

Design and make a class Christmas book.

Examine pop up books and cards and then make one of your own.

Compare the different styles of illustration used in books of the past e.g. story books, old Bibles etc. Work in the style of one of these illustrations.

Examine books on special subjects e.g. gardening, cookery, fishing etc. Design a cover and title for one to be reprinted.

INDIVIDUAL ACTIVITIES

Make clay tablets of simple text.

Copy a passage from a special book using quill and ink.

Research, design and create your own illuminated letter.

Make a Hebrew Scroll.

Make printing blocks from materials such as potato, polystyrene sheet, cardboard etc. Experiment with these.

Print pictures and text.

Try printing with a "John Bull" type printing set.

Make a special book of your own - bind and decorate the cover.

END PRODUCT

Display of written and creative work or individual booklets made.

Display of favourite books and comments about why they are special to some individuals.

Large frieze showing scenes from a story found in a holy book.

Class assembly/drama work telling the story of the underground Bible movement or the story of Mary Jones.

Make a large 3D relief map of the Bible lands.

Create a special place in the classroom to keep the classes own book.

Act out a special book story e.g. Joseph and his coat of many colours.

PROGRAMME OF STUDY

Pupils should be taught:
- to design and make simple products
- carry out practical tasks in which they develop and practice particular skills and knowledge (in this case
- how structures can fail when loaded, and techniques for reinforcing and strengthening them)
- take part in activities in which they investigate, disassemble and evaluate simple products
- work with a range of materials and components
- work independently and in teams
- apply skills, knowledge and understanding from other subjects e.g. The following is from the science programme
- that forces act in particular directions
- that forces acting on an object can balance, e.g. *in a tug of war, on a floating object*, and that when this happens an object at rest stays still

SKILLS TO BE DEVELOPED

Designing Skills
- generate ideas
- clarify ideas and suggest ways forward
- consider appearance, function, safety and reliability
- model ideas to explore aspects of the design
- evaluate design ideas and look for improvements
- develop a clear idea of what has to be done

Making Skills
- select appropriate materials, tools and techniques
- measure, mark out, cut and shape a range of materials using appropriate tools and equipment
- join and combine materials and components accurately in temporary and permanent ways
- apply finishing techniques appropriate to the purpose of the product
- evaluate the product by carrying out appropriate tests
- implement improvements identified as being necessary

SUPPORTING CURRICULUM LINKS

English	-	Write an adventure story in which a bridge is central to the plot
Maths	-	Use a clinometer to measure the heights of bridges and towers
Science	-	Work on strength of materials and forces in structures
History	-	Research the history of some famous bridges e.g. Golden Gate, Forth Rail Bridge etc.
Geography	-	Debate building a motorway bridge in a local beauty spot
P.E.	-	Make bridge shapes with your body.

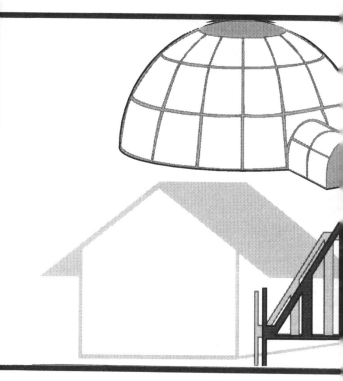

WHOLE CLASS ACTIVITIES

Learn how tests can be carried out on different materials. Test some simple structures to destruction. Tilt tables holding structures and discuss the effects of gravity. Discuss why structures are often wider at the bottom than the top. Talk about spanning large distances. Talk about the forces involved in all of these.

Learn how to make structures with Jinks' Triangles, or glueing lolly sticks to strip/dowel/square section wood using a cool glue gun.

Learn how to make structures with art straws, bendy drinking straws, Corriflute, Correx, pipe cleaners etc.

Learn how to make card and paper structures stronger by folding and making tubes.

Experiment with triangulated meccano strips or with structures made from other construction kits e.g. Beaver (Uni-Lab in Blackburn, Lancs), Brio-mec, Teko (which is square section wood with plastic joints and gears).

SMALL GROUP ACTIVITIES

Agree exactly what is to be built in a permanent way in groups e.g. a bridge or a tower; a bridge between two bricks 30cm or 60cm or 1m apart to carry a load of say 200g etc.

Discuss the construction and individually draw designs. Debate with the help of an adult the best design points to be used.

Finalise the design, allocate tasks and collect materials.

Build the model, test it and look for improvements.

STARTING POINTS

Make visits to bridges/towers/pylons/adventure playgrounds in the local environment. Look for patterns in the structures. Sketch and take photographs.

Make a collection of pictures/books which show bridges from around the world and in the past.

Discuss materials used and patterns observed in real structure. Compare with materials available for models e.g. string for a model suspension bridge.

Decide between bridges or towers to construct.

Recommended Reference Books
Science in a Topic - "Roads, Bridges and Tunnels" - Hulton.

RESOURCES/EQUIPMENT

Card, artstraws, glue, paper, scissors, safety snips, weights, sticky tape, string, newspapers, etc.

Construction kits e.g. Lego, Connect-a-Straw, Meccano etc.

Possible Visits
Local motorway/railway/river bridges.
Local Towers etc.
Bridges built by youth teams to improve areas.

Possible Visitors
Territorial Army to build a bridge in the school yard. Civil Engineers from local council.

Best Time of Year
Any.

Design and Make:
Simple
Structures
(forces and motion)

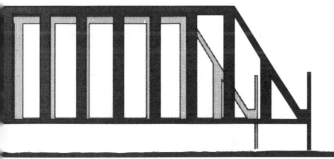

ART AND DISPLAY

Display pictures of different types of bridges including bridges in Art e.g. Hackney, Monet's Water-Garden Bridge, Whistler etc.

Make observational drawings of local bridges.

Make a model of a bridge included in a work of art.

Design and draw an imaginery bridge.

Display photographs of famous towers e.g. Blackpool Tower, Eiffel Tower, Tower of Pizza etc.

Make silhouettes of towers against a sunset/stormy sky.

Focus on patterns found within a pylon. Collect and draw different designs. Develop into a repeating pattern using black paper strips. Colour with crayons or paint.

INDIVIDUAL ACTIVITIES

Work with a range of materials e.g. newspaper, artstraws, corriflute, magazines, string, card, wood, junk etc.

Devise and carry out a fair test to find out:
i)   Which materials are easily cut.
ii) Which materials are easily joined.
iii) Which are the strongest materials.
iv) Which are the most flexible materials.

Use this information in your choice of materials used for building your structure.

END PRODUCT

A model bridge which will span an agreed gap.

A model bridge which will hold an agreed weight.

A model bridge which an agreed model car can pass over.

A model bridge attractively finished off made to look as real as possible.

A model tower built from a limited range of materials.

The tallest/strongest/most stable model tower.

PROGRAMME OF STUDY

In studying rivers and their effects on the landscape, pupils should be taught:

- that rivers have sources, channels, tributaries and mouths, that they receive water from a wide area, and that most eventually flow into a lake or the sea
- how rivers erode, transport and deposit materials, producing particular landscape features e.g. *valleys, waterfalls*

This study can be set within the context of the European Union.

SKILLS TO BE DEVELOPED

- observe and question about geographical features and issues, collect/record evidence to answer questions, analyse, draw conclusions and communicate findings
- use appropriate geographical vocabulary to describe and interpret their surroundings
- undertake fieldwork using appropriate instruments
- make maps and plans at a variety of scales
- use and interpret globes, and maps and plans at a variety of scales; the work should include using co-ordinates and four-figure grid references, measuring direction and distance, following routes, using the contents page and index of an atlas, and identifying the points of reference specified on the Geog. N.C. maps
- use secondary sources of evidence to provide information e.g. pictures; photographs (including aerial photographs) T.V.; radio; books; newspapers; visitors
- use IT to gain access to additional information sources and to assist in handling, classifying and presenting evidence

SUPPORTING CURRICULUM LINKS

English - Write poems about rushing/ gurgling/moving water. Write a "James Bond" type adventure involving a chase across Europe using various means of transport. Listen to simple language tapes and learn a few "French" words. Write letters to a class in a continental school. Listen to "The Wheel on the School" by Meindert de Jong.

Maths - Research European currencies and calculate how much of each you could exchange for £1.

Science - Filter/evaporate river water.

Technology - Design and sketch an alternative to the channel tunnel.

History - Research the history of the E.E.C.

Music - Listen/learn/comment on some traditional music.

R.E. - Sketch and name some European places of worship.

P.E. - Movement based on channel tunnel excavations.

WHOLE CLASS ACTIVITIES

Learn names to describe parts of a river e.g. source, channels, tributaries and mouth etc.

Talk about river erosion/deposition and the resulting effects.

Learn about the water cycle.

Organise groups to model sections of a river.

Make individual political maps of Europe (National Curriculum Map B) plotting the course of the Rhine. Discuss how many different countries border the river.

Examine pictures and photographs of the Rhine. Discuss its use as a major trade and tourist route.

Learn about the port of Rotterdam.

Talk about trade and the different types of cargo that are carried on the Rhine.

Define the terms Europe and E.E.C.

SMALL GROUP ACTIVITIES

Make a model of one part of a river to link with other groups to make a whole class model.

Make a large model of a Rhine cargo barge.

Plan a holiday to a European country. Choose a destination, plan what to take, how to get there and how much it will cost.

Design a travel brochure for a European holiday. Include details about travel, where to stay, itinerary, route and high/low season costs.

Use maps to plot a journey across Europe e.g. Orient Express. Name the countries passed through, describe the scenery and the time taken.

Use slides/postcards/photographs to compare scenes in one country with your own area.

Use latitude and longitude to locate European places in an atlas.

STARTING POINTS

Demonstrate the action of a river by pouring water from a watering can over a sand hill.

Demonstrate erosion by pouring water over a large rock covered with sand, gravel and soil.

Visit a nearby river or stream to measure for drawings/ model of a cross-section. Look for evidence of erosion.

Make a collection and talk about holiday souvenirs, travel brochures, European football teams, newspaper cuttings, national dolls etc.

Construct a giant map of Europe with groups contributing individual countries drawn to same scale and fitted together like a jig-saw.

Make a large 3D model of Europe showing seas, main mountain regions and national boundaries.

Recommended Reference Books

Rivers - Terry Jennings - O.U.P.
Usborne Nature Trail Books of Ponds and Streams.
Europe - Maps and Mapwork - Macmillan Education.
The World - Maps and Mapwork - Macmillan Education.
Usborne Guides to France, Spain etc.
Usborne Picture Word Books - French, German etc.

RESOURCES/EQUIPMENT

A collection of postcards and photographs. Atlases and globes.
Continental Newspapers.
Micro Map 1 and 2 - Computer Program which practices map reading skills - Longman.
P.C.E.T. wall charts - River Pollution.
The River Water Pack - produced by WATCH - Richmond Publishing.

Possible Visits
Take a coach and follow the route of a local river from source to mouth. Take a day trip to Rotterdam.

Possible Visitors
An officer from the National Rivers Authority to talk about their work. A fisherman or amateur naturalist to talk about life along the river bank.

Best Time of Year
Any.

Rhine - River of Europe

ART AND DISPLAY

Collect pictures of the Rhine/barges/scenery along banks etc.

Make a 3D class model based on one of these views.

Design a poster/brochure to encourage a holiday on a Rhine cruise.

Make a 3D model of a Rhine barge.

Draw a picture of an imaginary castle set in the mountains along the river.

Draw pictures of yourself and a friend dressed as tourists to go on a boat trip.

Make observational drawings of objects that have been brought back from the region around the Rhine - food/ drink etc.

Make several patterns using the colours of the German flag.

Copy designs from European food wrappings.

INDIVIDUAL ACTIVITIES

Make a map showing where Europe is in the world.

Plot a route from your locality to Rotterdam.

Define the terms source; confluence; gorge; meander; alluvium; ox-bow lake; delta.

Research everyday way of life, jobs, foods eaten, housing, spare time activity, homes etc. in one European country.

Research how climate varies across Europe and discuss how this effects the way of life.

Make drawings/paintings of famous landmarks, national flags, national dress etc.

Paint designs on plates from continental pottery.

Answer quiz questions using an atlas.

Learn to play the French game of boules.

Make a map of European air routes.

END PRODUCT

Completed class model showing parts of a river.

Individual topic booklets containing stories written and information collected.

Large class map of one European country containing rivers, mountains, cities etc.

A continental meal or food tasting session.

Make a large scale mock up of the channel tunnel with a model railway.

Hold a competition to see who can build a model ferry which will hold more cars than any other.

Make a collage of a busy port.

Make a frieze of a typical rural dutch scene.

Make a working model of a roll-on roll-off ferry terminal.

PROGRAMME OF STUDY

Pupils should be taught:
- to compare everyday materials, e.g. *wood, rock, iron, aluminium, paper, polythene*, on the basis of their properties, including hardness, strength, flexibility and magnetic behaviour, and to relate these properties to everyday uses of the materials
- to describe and group rocks and soils on the basis of characteristics, including appearance, texture and permeability
- to recognise differences between solids, liquids and gases, in terms of ease of flow and maintenance of shape and volume
- that solid particles of different sizes, e.g. *those in soils*, can be separated by sieving
- that some solids, e.g. *salt, sugar*, dissolve in water to give solutions but some, e.g. *sand, chalk*, do not
- that insoluble solids can be separated from liquids by filtering
- that solids that have dissolved can be recovered by evaporating the liquid from the solution
- that there is a limit to the mass of solid that can dissolve in a given amount of water, and that this limit is different for different solids
- that the changes that occur when most materials, e.g. *wood, wax, natural gas*, are burned are not reversible.

SKILLS TO BE DEVELOPED

- to be able to turn ideas suggested to them, and their own ideas, into a form that can be investigated
- to know that making predictions can be useful when planning what to do
- to decide what evidence should be collected
- to know that changing one factor and observing and measuring the effect, whilst keeping other factors the same, allows a fair test or comparison to be made
- to consider what apparatus and equipment to use
- to use simple apparatus and equipment correctly
- to make careful observations and measurements
- to check observations and measurements by repeating them
- to use tables, bar charts and line graphs to present results
- to make comparisons and to identify trends or patterns in results
- to use results to draw conclusions
- to indicate whether the evidence collected supports any prediction made
- to try to explain conclusions in terms of scientific knowledge and understanding

SUPPORTING CURRICULUM LINKS

English	-	Make a word bank to describe the physically observable properties of solids, liquids and gases. Make a list of materials and how mankind uses them.
Maths	-	Measure quantities of ingredients to make custard and jelly.
Technology	-	Design and build a funnel to hold filter paper out of junk materials. Design and build a machine to test the hardness of a solid.
History	-	Research how glass was first made.
Geography	-	Use maps to trace the sources of some everyday materials.
P.E.	-	Make solid/liquid/gas type movements.

WHOLE CLASS ACTIVITIES

Talk about rocks and soils as raw materials for man to use. Describe and group examples of both on the basis of their characteristics.

Talk about permanent and temporary change.

Solids: List as many solids as possible. Talk about solids that change when heated. Ask if they return to original state or is the change permanent? e.g. chocolate, candle wax, toast, eggs etc.

Liquids: Talk about liquids and solutions. How do liquids change when heated? Do they return to original state? Make ice. Shake double cream to make cheese. Demonstrate how filtration can separate solids from liquids. Mix plaster of paris and observe how it turns into a solid.

Gases: Talk about air and the gases that make it up. Show air trapped in a tumbler under water. Burn a candle in a sealed jam jar. Demonstrate how to make carbon dioxide and how to test for it.

Demonstrate how liquids fill jars but solids leave gaps. Talk about the effects of burning are not reversible.

SMALL GROUP ACTIVITIES

Make a dish of custard and jelly. Observe and record the processes involved and the changes that take place.

Devise a fair test to compare some common everyday materials e.g. wood, rock, iron, aluminium, paper, polythene, etc. on the basis of their properties including hardness, strength, flexibility and magnetic behaviour.

Experiment with:
Boiling water and melting ice.
Simple chemical reactions, e.g. baking powder with vinegar and water.
Dissolving materials in water.
Saturation of different solutions.
Separating soil from dirty water using filtration.
Separating a mixture of sand and salt using filtration and evaporation.
Useful properties of materials, e.g. appropriate materials for constructing an umbrella.

STARTING POINTS

Define the term "material".
List as many materials as the class can think of and try to group into natural and man-made.

Define the term "change".
Talk about how man changes materials to create useful everyday objects e.g. how a tree is changed into a wooden chair or stool.

Define the term "chemical".
Talk about how man uses materials found naturally and changes them through chemical reactions to form new materials e.g. making iron in a blast furnace.

Recommended Reference Books
The Young Scientist Investigates - Everyday Chemicals - Published by Oxford University Press.
Science in the Kitchen - Usborne Books.

RESOURCES/EQUIPMENT

Jam jars, blotting or filter papers, candles, a selection of "safe" powders and solutions, samples of different rocks and soils etc.

Materials and Change - Photocopiable experiments and investigations - Pub. by Topical Resources.

P.C.E.T. Wallcharts "Structures and Materials".

Possible Visits
A bakery, a local chemical works, a secondary school science laboratory, a chemist's shop, a furniture manufacturer etc.

Possible Visitors
A pharmacist or doctor to talk about the use of chemicals in their work.
A woodworker to talk about why different woods are used for a variety of purposes.

Best Time of Year
Any.

Materials & Change

ART AND DISPLAY

Make collections of coloured materials e.g. textured, black and white, different types of paper, hard/soft materials, natural/man-made etc.

Display in squares as a patchwork or inside a box.

Work with materials that change during their use e.g. powder paint, liquid paint, clay, plaster of paris, modroc, papier mache etc. Change materials by bending, gluing, painting, cutting, joining etc.

Make a series of patterns which record a slice of tomato as it rots away.

Design a poster to make people aware of the chemical dangers in the home.

Make observational drawings of rock surfaces.

Make plaster casts of patterns drawn in old plasticine.

Make plaster cast models from rubber moulds.

INDIVIDUAL ACTIVITIES

Research and make annotated drawings showing how one everyday object is made from raw materials.

Compare clay, peat and sand by feel, smell, rolling and ability to pass through a sieve.

Make your own soil from the ingredients of: sand, mud, peat, gravel and rock fragments, seeds and old leaves.

Observe wire wool rusting half in and half out of water over several days.

Use dictionaries and reference books to define the terms: solid, liquid, gas.

Identify "SAFE" mystery powders by observation, smelling and mixing with water.

Send messages to a friend using invisible ink (fresh lemon juice - heat in oven to see message).

END PRODUCT

Make a change chart - a classroom chart which lists every "change" discovered during the topic.

Display examples of naturally occuring and man-made materials.

Make up individual topic booklets containing written accounts of visits/observations made and research carried out.

Display crystals made from a chemical solution.

Make a display of single substances and mixtures.

Hold a smelling quiz!

PROGRAMME OF STUDY

Pupils should be taught about the lives of men, women and children at different levels of society in Britain and the ways in which they were affected by changes in industry and transport:
- steam power, factories and mass production, e.g. *economic growth and the provision of jobs for men and women, the impact of mass production on living and working conditions*
- the growth of railways, e.g. *the work of Robert Stephenson and Isambard Kingdom Brunel, the impact of railways on everyday life*
- at work, e.g. *factory life, Lord Shaftesbury and factory reform, Florence Nightingale and nursing, domestic service, agriculture, the armed forces, the merchant marine, workhouses*
- at home e.g. *family life at different levels of society, Victoria and the royal family, the role of religion, public health and medicine*
- at leisure e.g. *music, sport, holidays, the Great Exhibition*
- at school e.g. *Sunday Schools, voluntary schools, board schools, public schools.*

SKILLS TO BE DEVELOPED

- to be able to place events, people and changes in periods studied within a chronological framework
- to be able to use dates and terms relating to the passing of time, including ancient, modern, BC, AD, century and decade
- to have an understanding of the characteristic features of particular periods and societies
- to be able to describe and identify reasons for and the results of main events and changes in the periods studied and make links across periods
- to be able to identify and give reasons for different ways in which the past is represented and interpreted
- to be able to find out about aspects of the periods studied from a range of sources of information including documents and printed sources, artefacts, pictures and photographs, music and buildings and sites
- to know the terms necessary to describe the periods and topics studied, including court, monarch, parliament, nation, civilisations, invasion, conquest, settlement, conversion, slavery, trade, industry, law.

SUPPORTING CURRICULUM LINKS

English	-	Write "If I were Queen - I would change ...".
Maths	-	Problems with pounds, shillings and pence.
Science	-	Investigate how a steam engine works and the uses made of the invention.
Technology	-	Design and build a water powered mill wheel.
Geography	-	Examine maps of the British Empire. Find out names of present countries.
P.E.	-	Try a P.E. lesson based on "drill".
Music	-	Act out a scene from a music hall.
R.E.	-	Discuss working children and their working conditions. Discuss the changes Lord Shaftebury's reforms made to them.

WHOLE CLASS ACTIVITIES

Talk about different ways of finding out about the past e.g. from books, photographs, paintings, old newspapers, documents, novels, census returns, artefacts, oral evidence etc.

Devise a set of questions to ask an older member of the community that was born at the turn of the century. If possible, sensitively carry out an interview.

Talk about the invention of the railways and the changes this made to ordinary lives.

Run a model steam engine in the classroom and discuss what it needs to work. Talk about uses in railways, farming, ships and factories. Talk about expansion of industry in towns.

Dress in Victorian dress for a day/morning. Act out a classroom scene. Write on slates, chant tables etc. Write with pen and ink in well using joined up style.

Do simple sums with pounds, shillings and pence etc. Play appropriate playground games.

Visit an area which contains "Victorian" and contemporary architecture - compare and note the differences.

Listen to a class novel based in the time. Illustrate or write descriptions of some of the scenes.

SMALL GROUP ACTIVITIES

Study photographs and period drawings made in late Victorian times and note similarities and differences from present times.

Study pictures of people in the workhouse. Attempt to interpret what workers/supervisors are thinking about the same situation.

Look at advertisements in old newspapers to find the types of goods sold and prices charged.

Study one particular street or locality. Find old photographs, maps, plans, census information etc. Try to build up a picture of one particular family. Make models of the houses lived in.

Make a time line which shows important events and inventions.

Match Victorian artefacts to modern equivalents.
Make a quiz about Queen Victoria's family tree.
Make lists of facts about Victorian times. Compare with a list of opinions. Use this knowledge when studying other historical documents.

STARTING POINTS

Watch extracts from I.T.V. video - Victorians.
Visit a local museum with a Victorian theme.
Learn how to extract information from a computer data base on a Victorian theme.
Dress a child in Victorian costume and use as model for class to draw.
Make a collection of Victorian artefacts and talk about their uses.
Make a class time line to show where "Victorian Times" fit into historical order.
Discuss some of the main events and changes in Victorian Times.

Recommended Reference Books
Queen Anne to Queen Victoria - R.J. Unstead - Pub. by A & C Black (still an excellent resource!)
How We Used to Live 1850-1901 - F. Kelsall - Pub. by Simon and Schuster.
Two Victorian Families - S. Wagstaff - Pub. by A & C Black.
The Victorians - Pub. by Ladybird.
The Photocopiable Victorian Activity Book - Pub. by Topical Resources.

RESOURCES/EQUIPMENT

Census data taken from 1841, 1851, 1861, 1871, 1881 and 1891. Old photographs, etchings, artefacts etc.
Reproduction Victorian O.S. maps and street plans.
Reproduction newspapers and postcards.
I.T.V. How We Used to Live Video 1874-1887.
P.C.E.T. Wall Charts Early Victorians and Late Victorians.
Philip Green A4 picture pack - Victorians.
I.T. - B.B.C. Educational Publishing - The Victorians.

Possible Visits
Wigan Pier Museum, a Victorian Cottage, Victorian Mansion or any "Victorian Theme" museum. An area of town/city where Victorian architecture predominates or an antique shop.

Possible Visitors
The Curator of a local museum or museum Education Officer.
A local historian or antiques dealer.

Best Time of Year
Any

Victorian Britain

ART AND DISPLAY

Make a collection of Victorian artefacts for display e.g. oil or paraffin lamps, bottles, kitchen tools, flat iron etc. Use for observational drawing.

Study William Morris designs - past to present - produced from observational drawings of a plant. Make own design and use for wallpaper. Make a shoe box into a Victorian front room.

Draw popular Victorian plants e.g. Aspidistra, Maiden Hair, Fern. Leaf shapes could be developed into pattern work using silhouettes.

Look at Tissot's paintings for upper class costume. Paint yourself wearing one of these costumes.

Make drawings of lace and develop them into a large scale colour composition.

Look for repeating patterns in Victorian architecture e.g. railings - windows - ridge tiles etc. Use as a border design in cut paper.

Look at the designs for around fireplaces - design a set of tiles of your own.

Trace profiles on O.H.P. to create cameo silhouettes.

INDIVIDUAL ACTIVITIES

Interview people at home for memories or stories handed down from Victorian times. Write in pentagons, decorate with border and display as a patchwork quilt.

Make sample rag rugs.

Research the conditions in mills; Florence Nightingale; Lord Shaftebury; changes in transport etc.

Make a map of the British Empire.

Make a model Zoetrope.

Study entries in a school log book and school rules of the time.

Construct a model Music Hall/Theatre - use cut out figures on wire to act out a play.

Examine unusual Victorian artefacts and speculate about their use.

Cut out clothes to dress a card outline Victorian Doll - research appropriate colours and materials to make the dresses as accurate as possible.

END PRODUCT

Collect sketches, drawings and paintings made and create a collage of "Victoriana".

Make up individual booklets of research carried out, stories written, visits made etc.

Hold a Victorian fashion parade.

Hold a Victorian Day. Dress in appropriate costume and act out a school day/morning with copper plate writing and maths in £,s,d.

Create a full size Victorian shop front.

Make a model Victorian street scene with rows of terraced cottages, a factory building, shops, one or two Victorian mansions and appropriate street transport.

Make a collection of Victorian toys or artefacts displayed as if in a museum.

PROGRAMME OF STUDY

Pupils should be taught:
- that there are life processes, including nutrition, movement, growth and reproduction, common to animals
- how locally occurring animals and plants can be identified and assigned to groups, using keys.
- that different plants and animals are found in different habitats
- how animals and plants in different habitats are suited to their environment
- that food chains show feeding relationships in an ecosystem
- that nearly all food chains start with a green plant
- that micro-organisms exist, and that many may be beneficial, e.g. *in the breakdown of waste*, while others may be harmful, e.g. *in causing disease.*

SKILLS TO BE DEVELOPED

- to ask questions e.g. How; Why; What will happen if?
- to know how to use first hand experience and simple secondary sources to obtain information
- to be able to relate understanding of science to domestic and environmental contexts
- to consider ways in which science is related to personal health
- to learn how to treat living things and the environment with care and sensitivity
- to relate simple scientific ideas to the evidence for them
- to use scientific vocabulary to name and describe living things, materials, phenomena and processes
- to present scientific information in a number of ways e.g. through drawings, diagrams, tables and charts, and in speech and writing
- to recognise hazards and risks when working with living things and materials
- to follow simple instructions to control the risks to themsevles.

SUPPORTING CURRICULUM LINKS

English	-	List words/write poems to describe insect movement. Create a story about "life at the bottom of the pond" giving creatures names and characters. Debate: "Filling in ponds to create more farm land."
Maths	-	Calculate area of pond surfaces
History	-	Research one prehistoric amphibian
Geography	-	Locate ponds using local O.S. maps. Map the route to the local pond
I.T.	-	Use an appropriate data base to research facts about individual pond creatures
P.E.	-	Movement - Act out insect movement.
R.E.	-	Research the Christian use of fish symbol.

WHOLE CLASS ACTIVITIES

Discuss the concept of a "Habitat" and in particular a "Freshwater Habitat".

Discuss common animals, plants and birds found in and around a freshwater habitat.

Learn the difference between vertebrates and invertebrates.

Discuss life cycles and predator-prey relationships.

Make examples of simple food chains.

Talk about how micro-organisms help to maintain life in a pond.

Plan and collect together equipment needed for the exploration of a small watery habitat. Visit a local habitat and carry out planned investigations. Return to classroom with appropriate samples, notes and sketches. Set up a "mini-environment" in a tank in the classroom. Return to source after 2 or 3 weeks.

Demonstrate how to use a binocular microscope and binoculars. Demonstrate and practice with class games how to use a simple scientific key.

SMALL GROUP ACTIVITIES

Use a simple scientific key to identify pond creatures.

Make first hand close up observations of pond creatures (the teacher should emphasise the sensitive collection and care of living things). To do this, use a dropper or fine paint brush to take samples from the class tank and observe using magnified specimen jar or under a binocular microscope. Make sketches and descriptions of observations made.

Use pictures and reference books to identify some common pond plants and water birds.

STARTING POINTS

This study should focus if at all possible on a local watery habitat. Examples include a school pond, a parent's pond, a park/wild pond, a slow moving stream, a clean stretch of canal or a sea-side rock pool. The topic should be named appropriately.

Discuss the topic and make plans for a study. Visit a pond to look. Visit again to collect samples. Set up a pond type environment in the classroom.

If unable to visit a pond, recreate an imaginary pond in the classroom with pupils making model pond creatures.

Recommended Reference Books
The Nature Trail Book of Ponds and Streams - Usborne Books.
The Photocopiable Pond Activity Book - Topical Resources (contains appropriate Scientific Key).
The Pondwatch Pack - Wildfowl and Wetlands Trust.

RESOURCES/EQUIPMENT

A collection of reference books; a simple scientific key; binocular microscope; binoculars; specimen holders; plastic tank, air pump and filter etc. various fishing nets.

Philip Green A4 Colour Picture Pack - Pond Life.
P.C.E.T. Poster - The Frog.

Computer Program - "Just Pictures - Pond Life" available from Semerc Dealers.

Possible Visits
A local watery habitat.

Possible Visitors
Conservation volunteer, a local gardener with a pond.

Best Time of Year
Summer term or early September for maximum pond life.

In a Pond

ART AND DISPLAY

Insects/plants/fish and water patterns - collect pictures of all.

Make observational drawings of any actually collected. e.g. Iris-balrushes etc.

Look at reflections - in water and produce a symmetrical image in cut paper - develop patterns/ colours in water into a large scale abstract design.

Look at Claude Monet's many paintings of the pond in his garden at Givenchy.

Look at dragon flies as a shape for design - a repeating pattern - as used in Tiffany glass designs.

Make cut out silhouettes of different shapes of water beetles.

Use the pattern on fish to develop a pattern in a group of colour related repeating shapes.

Design an imaginary creature to live in a pond.

INDIVIDUAL ACTIVITIES

Research the life processes of a fish, an amphibian, a bird and an insect which spends its young life in water and adult life in the air.

Make life-cycle dials which show simply the life cycle of one pond creature.

Design and make simple pond dipping nets.

Experiment with animal camouflage and relate this to life in a pond.

Experiment with water tension and relate this to life in a pond.

END PRODUCT

Plan and build a pond in the school grounds. Plant and stock appropriately. Fence off for safety.

Make up individual topic booklets containing written accounts of visits/observations made and research carried out.

Make a display of models made.

Make a large frieze/cross-section showing where different pond creatures would be found in and around a watery habitat.

Create a "model" wildlife pond in the classroom. Invite infant children/parents/headteacher for a guided tour.

PROGRAMME OF STUDY

Question the meaning of "a leader".

Question the meaning of "a teacher".

Who is my teacher? What am I taught? How did my teacher become a teacher? Groups of people called Christians have a teacher called Jesus; Buddhists the Buddha; Sikhs have ten great Gurus or 'teachers' the first being Guru Nanak; Muslims have a Prophet called Muhammad.

Children should learn about the life story of Jesus and other religious teachers. They should learn a little of the fundamental teaching of Christians/other religions how their God is to be worshipped and the sort of life followers are expected to lead.

SKILLS TO BE DEVELOPED

Study religious beliefs and practices and relate them to one's own experience.

Enter imaginatively into the motivations, feelings, responses, experiences, hopes, aspirations, beliefs, values, attitudes and perceptions of religious believers. (Planning R.E. in Schools - C.E.M.)

Think deeply about and question sensitive aspects of human experience.

SUPPORTING CURRICULUM LINKS

English	-	Make a list of the qualities a leader has. Write a newspaper report of an event which took place in a religious teachers life.
Maths	-	Study N.T. weights, measures and systems of money.
Technology	-	Design a container to be sealed, protect documents and be re-opened in 2000 years time. List possible contents.
History	-	Construct a time-line showing when various leaders lived.
Geography	-	Mark on world map where religious teachers taught.
Music	-	Listen to and talk about music from Buddhist/Sikh/Islamic cultures.
P.E./Drama	-	Role play a situation in which a leader is to emerge from a group.

WHOLE CLASS ACTIVITIES

Talk about the fact that many people in the world hold a religious belief (a believer); some are undecided (agnostic) and some have reasoned that there is no God (atheist).

Talk about how Christians see Jesus as the son of God, who came to the earth to teach people how to find God and how he eventually returned to heaven.

Talk about how Buddha was born of a wealthy family and how he devoted his life to finding the answer to the world's sufferings.

Talk about the ten great Gurus of the Sikh religion, each having equal importance, the first being Guru Nanak.

Talk about Muhammed as the last in a series of 26 prophets belonging to Islam.

Talk about what is meant by prayer.

Talk about a parable and relate it to present day life.

Talk about miracles and speculate what they mean/how they happened. If possible get an expert in to assist with this.

SMALL GROUP ACTIVITIES

Individually, in pairs, in groups and finally as a whole class devise a list of rules for the world to live by.

Compare your list with suggestions from some world faiths. Talk about how the suggestions vary.

Use children's Bibles to read about, examine and think about some of the teachings of Jesus. Include a miracle and a parable.

Use shadow puppets to recreate a chosen story which may need to be adapted for this form of presentation.

Practise, perfect and finally use the Shadow Puppet Stories in a class assembly or a video T.V. programme.

Make large 3D maps of Palestine constructing papier-mache hills.

Make a group collage depicting a scene from a leaders life.

STARTING POINTS

Explore the idea of "what is a teacher" by looking up dictionary/encyclopedia definitions and then making a list of interview questions.

Interview a teacher to find out what you have to do to become a school teacher, what the work involves, why they chose to do it etc.

Make lists of other kinds of teachers e.g. music teacher, car maintenance teacher, etc.

Talk abut who Christians believe taught them about God. Was he a trained teacher?

Books
The Lion (hardback) or the Puffin (paperback) Children's Bible - retold by Pat Alexander
Religious Teachers and Prophets - J. Mayled - Wayland
Exploring a theme - Leaders - C.E.M.

RESOURCES/EQUIPMENT

Dictionary; Encyclopedia; School Library; Slides; Videos; etc.
P.C.E.T. wallchart - "My Neighbour's Religion".
A good collection of children's reference books which touch on the theme.
A class set of children's Bibles.
Various pictures depicting Christ. Pictures/music from Buddhist, Sikh, Islamic cultures.

Possible Visits
Visit a relevant place of worship not previously visited.

Possible Visitors
A Christian/Buddhist/Sikh/Islam believer to talk about a religious leader.

Leaders & Teachers

ART AND DISPLAY

Paint portraits of the school staff.

Make a collage of the interests/hobbies of a particular teacher.

Make sketches of mum, grandparents, cub leaders etc - others that teach us things.

Design a school uniform for a teacher.

Paint pictures or make a collage of portraits of people who lead the country in one way or another e.g. The Queen, Primeminister etc.

Examine badges/hats/uniforms worn by leaders of different organisations. Design a new badge/hat/ uniform for an imaginary organisation.

Look at coats of arms and their designs in relation to whom they belong. Design a coat of arms for your family.

INDIVIDUAL ACTIVITIES

Research and write a simple account of the life story of Jesus, Buddha, Guru Nanak or Muhammed.

Paint a portrait of Jesus by copying an old painting or a more contemporary impression.

Make a model house from Bible times.

Sketch/paint someone dressed in traditional Bible costume.

Draw a map of Palestine marking on key towns and villages.

Make clay models of Buddha.

Take a teaching from one leader and write in your own words what it means to you.

END PRODUCT

Display of written and creative work or individual booklets made.

Class assembly based on work with shadow puppets.

A class definition of the qualities of a good religious leader.

Make a booklet showing main events in life of each leader studied.

Make a frieze/collage of one event from the life of each leader studied.

Discuss why Jesus was a good leader and a good teacher.

PROGRAMME OF STUDY

Pupils should be taught:
- to design and make simple products
- carry out practical tasks in which they develop and practice particular skills and knowledge (in this case - how different ingredients can be combined and mixed in order to create attractive and tasty meals)
- take part in activities in which they investigate, disassemble and evaluate simple products
- work with a range of materials and components
- work independently and in teams
- apply skills, knowledge and understanding from other subjects e.g. The following is from the science programme of study
- that mixing materials, e.g. adding salt to water, can cause them to change
- that heating or cooling materials, e.g. water, clay, dough, can cause them to change, and that temperature is a measure of how hot or cold they are
- that some changes can be reversed and some cannot
- that dissolving, melting, boiling, condensing, freezing and evaporating are changes that can be reversed

SKILLS TO BE DEVELOPED

Designing Skills
- generate ideas
- clarify ideas and suggest ways forward
- consider appearance, function, safety and reliability
- model ideas to explore aspects of the design
- evaluate design ideas and look for improvements
- develop a clear idea of what has to be done

Making Skills
- select appropriate materials, tools and techniques
- measure, mark out, cut and shape a range of materials using appropriate tools and equipment
- join and combine materials and components accurately in temporary and permanent ways
- apply finishing techniques appropriate to the purpose of the product
- evaluate the product by carrying out appropriate tests
- implement improvements identified as being necessary

SUPPORTING CURRICULUM LINKS

English	-	Write a report of the event for a "Food and Drink Magazine."
Maths	-	Weighing foods. Measuring liquids. Making accurate predictions of what is to be spent.
I.T.	-	Questionnaire for likes/dislikes. Design and print out menus.
Science	-	Talk about reversible and non-reversible changes. Health and Safety issues.
Geography	-	Research the countries of origin of some of the ingredients used.
History	-	Research foods used for a celebration in the past.
Music	-	Select appropriate background music to play at the event.

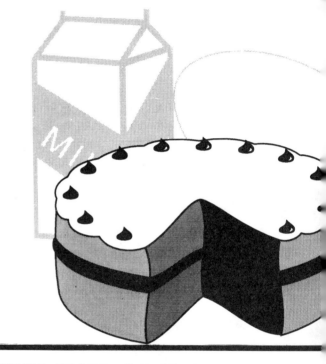

WHOLE CLASS ACTIVITIES

Discuss health and safety issues and write letters home to parents informing of the event.

Invite visitor/make a visit to taste unusual food. Update information stored in computer to include 'new' foods.

Learn how to make a basic biscuit recipe.

Learn how to make a basic cake recipe.

Discuss/experiment with the changes made by adding cherries, sultanas, coconut, chocolate drops, nuts, cocoa powder etc.

Discuss/experiment with finishes e.g. icing, marzipan, melted chocolate etc.

Compare oven/microwave cooking.

Agree on a menu for the celebration meal.

Agree about criteria for a successful outcome.

SMALL GROUP ACTIVITIES

Decide who is to cook which items.

List the ingredients required.

Create a shopping list for celebration food making it realistic for cost.

Visit local shops with rough draft of requirements to assess accurate costings and availability.

Adjust shopping list and make second visit to purchase the goods.

Store goods safely and decide when individual items are to be cooked and how they will be kept fresh previous to the event.

STARTING POINTS

Establish through discussion the occasion or event to be catered for. e.g. Christmas party, disco, leavers party, Summer/Autumn Fair etc.

Talk about how food is to be used as a raw material which will be changed e.g. mixed/joined, combined and finished.

Design individual questionnaires to find out favourite food and drinks. Carry out survey and compile information/enter into a computer data-base.

Visit a local supermarket to find out how food is delivered, handled and cared for on its way to the shelves.

Discuss variety of foods required for the celebration.

Recommended Reference Books
You and Your Child - Kitchen Fun - Usborne Books.
Usborne Introduction - You and Your Food.
The Usborne - First Cook Book.
Science in the Kitchen - Usborne Books.
Where Food Comes From - Usborne Books.

RESOURCES/EQUIPMENT

Baby belling/microwave oven.
Various tools for cutting, measuring, mixing and serving food.
Plates, cups, knives, forks, spoons etc.

Possible Visits
A local bakery or fast food restaurant.

Possible Visitors
Parents/friends from a variety of cultures.

Best Time of Year
Harvest, Christmas, Easter, Bonfire Night, Summer Picnic, End of School Year or any other occasion to celebrate.

Design and Make:
Food for a Celebration
(materials)

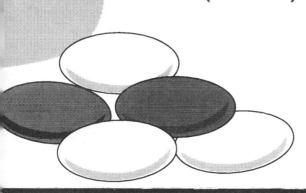

ART AND DISPLAY

Display designs for invitations, place mats, place names, serviettes etc. that reflect the occasion.

Display photographs of table settings, cookery books, menu designs.

Discuss coordinating colours and items that match.

Design the layout of a menu indicating the choice of food being offered for the celebration.

Fold, cut and make doilies coloured or white.

Look at meals in children's books and book illustrations.

Used dried foods for collage work.

INDIVIDUAL ACTIVITIES

Design and make an invitation, a place mat, a place name, a serviette, a menu which match and reflect the occasion.

Make, finish and display individual items of food. These may include: sandwiches with various fillings, jacket potatoes with various filling, pasta with added ingredients, cakes, biscuits, jelly, blancmange, meringues, ice lollies etc.

Store your food in an appropriate manner before the event.

Research the ingredients needed for a fruit cake. Use food packets/reference books to find countries of origin. Draw maps of routes travelled. Research transport used. Research how original crops are grown and the working conditions of the people who grow/pick the produce.

END PRODUCT

Produce a meal to celebrate an event displaying the end product attractively.

Invite younger children/parents/visitors to school to share the occasion.

Evaluate the meal produced against criteria agreed upon during the planning stage.

Clear up the remains disposing of left overs in an appropriate manner.

Write thank you letters to parents/friends that have helped provide the ingredients.

PROGRAMME OF STUDY

In studying how weather varies between places and over time, pupils should be taught:
- about the water cycle and the part played by evaporation and condensation
- how site conditions can influence the weather
- about seasonal weather patterns
- about weather conditions in different parts of the world. A distant locality should be studied. This should be similar in size to the locality of the school and come from a country in Africa, Asia (except Japan), South America or Central America (including the Caribbean).

Pupils should be taught:
- about the main physical and human features
- how this locality may be similar and how it may differ from home
- how the features of a locality influence the nature and location of human activities within it
- about recent and proposed changes in the locality
- how the locality is set within a broader geographical context and linked with other places.

SKILLS TO BE DEVELOPED

- observe and question about geographical features and issues, collect/record evidence to answer questions, analyse, draw conclusions and communicate findings
- use appropriate geographical vocabulary to describe and interpret their surroundings
- undertake fieldwork using appropriate instruments
- make maps and plans at a variety of scales
- use and interpret globes, and maps and plans at a variety of scales; the work should include using co-ordinates and four-figure grid references, measuring direction and distance, following routes, using the contents page and index of an atlas, and identifying the points of reference specified on the Geog. N.C. maps
- use secondary sources of evidence to provide information e.g. pictures; photographs (including aerial photographs) T.V.; radio; books; newspapers; visitors
- use IT to gain access to additional information sources and to assist in handling, classifying and presenting evidence.

SUPPORTING CURRICULUM LINKS

English	-	Collect examples and write your own poems about water. Write a story which involves extremes of weather e.g. A trip to the North Pole or A treck across the desert. Write a description of "Eating an ice-cream on a very hot day".
Maths	-	Measure accurately the volume of water collected after rain.
Science	-	Research where in the atmosphere 'weather' occurs.
Technology	-	Design and build a board game which uses latitude and longitude.
Music	-	Make music which represents different types of weather.
P.E.	-	Movement based on a fierce storm at sea.
R.E.	-	Discuss how the weather affects the way we feel.

WHOLE CLASS ACTIVITIES

Talk about the four seasons and demonstrate why they occur.
Talk about local features which affect the weather.
Talk about the wind and how it occurs. Demonstrate hot air rising.
Demonstrate the fact air has weight (two balloons on a balance) and this creates air pressure.
Examine globes and atlases. Locate places around the world with temperatures reported in the newspaper.
Talk about weather conditions at the equator, the tropics and the poles.
Choose a distant locality from Africa, Asia (except Japan), South America or Central America (including the Caribbean) to study. This will largely depend on the resources available to the class.
Locate your chosen locality on an atlas or globe.
Discuss the weather in your chosen locality.
Discuss how the climate influences the way of life.
Find out as much as you can about everyday life in your chosen locality.

SMALL GROUP ACTIVITIES

Compare your weather recordings with local weather forecasts - how often are they right?

Learn how to use a thermometer and make regular measurements of temperature.

Learn how to use a compass and make regular measurements of wind direction.

Use documents, books and photographs to research your distant locality. Find out what it is like to live there; how it compares with your own locality; the connections with other places; changes that are occuring and what people think of these etc.

Uses atlases to practice using lattitude and longitude.

Use nets to construct a globe from a flat sheet of card. Colour as a world map.

Make graphs and charts of your weather recordings. Talk about what they show.

STARTING POINTS

Encourage the children to talk about their own experiences of weather and then define the concept.

Talk about the three men elements - water, wind and heat.

Make own/use propriety weather measuring instruments e.g. thermometer, anenometer (wind speed), windvane or wind sock, rain guage etc. and set up a programme of weather recording. This may be done up to twelve monks before the study for maximum effect.

Demonstrate evaporation and condensation and talk about the rain cycle.

Recommended Reference Books
Weather Watch - Hodder and Stoughton.
A Spotter's Guide to the Weather - Usborne Books.
Usborne Science & Experiments - Weather & Climate.

RESOURCES/EQUIPMENT

A set of atlases and globes.
Thermometer, anemometer, wind vane, compass, rain gauge.
P.C.E.T. wall chart - The Weather and You.
A distant locality pack - a good example being the St. Lucia resources available from The Geographical Association.
I.T. Weather Station - record and display weather records and make weather forecasts - AVP.

Possible Visits
A weather station or T.V. studio which reports the weather. A coast guard station/life boat station which is influenced by the weather.

Possible Visitors
A weather forecaster; a coast guard or member of lifeboat crew or amateur yachtsman. A resident of your chosen distant locality or someone who has visited the area.

Best Time of Year
Any.

World Wide Weather
(including a distant locality)

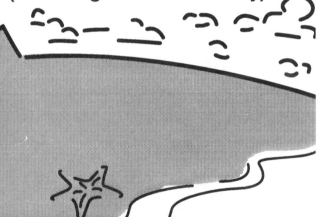

ART AND DISPLAY

Make a collection of pictures of different types of weather.

Design a weather symbol for each type of weather.

Look at clothing for different types of weather - design a set of ski wear, a swimming costume, a pair of sun glasses.

Look at the designs on umbrellas.

Make observational drawings of umbrellas.

Design a pattern of repeating weather symbols that could be used on an umbrella/sunshade. Look at hats for different weather conditions. Draw or paint your friend wearing one.

Paint a scene under a series of different weather conditions.

Paint e.g. unexpected weather at the North Pole.

INDIVIDUAL ACTIVITIES

Research the work of a Meteorologist.

Collect memories from members of your family about extreme weather conditions - find out how it affected their daily lives.

Define the terms: monsoon, hurricane, whirl wind, climatise.

Research erosion by wind, water and ice.

Plot temperatures in different parts of the world from newspaper cuttings.

Experiment with different materials to see which are most waterproof.

Illustrate the characteristic weather in each of the four seasons.

List the clothes you would wear in hot/cold weather. Design an outfit you would like to wear in each.

END PRODUCT

Individual topic booklets containing reports from experiments, information collected, stories written etc.

A display of the weather measuring instruments used with instructions on how to use them.

Charts and diagrams which illustrate the weather patterns measured locally and the temperatures recorded in different parts of the world.

A water-cycle frieze.

A distant locality display or fact sheet.

A holiday poster advertising the distant locality.

PROGRAMME OF STUDY

Pupils should be taught:
- that the Sun, Earth and Moon are approximately spherical
- that the position of the Sun appears to change during the day, and how shadows change as this happens
- that the Earth spins around its own axis, and how day and night are related to this spin
- that the Earth obits the Sun once each year, and that the Moon takes approximately 28 days to orbit the Earth
- that objects have weight because of the gravitational attraction between them and the Earth

SKILLS TO BE DEVELOPED

- to be able to turn ideas suggested to them, and their own ideas, into a form that can be investigated
- to know that making predictions can be useful when planning what to do
- to decide what evidence should be collected
- to know that changing one factor and observing and measuring the effect, whilst keeping other factors the same, allows a fair test or comparison to be made
- to consider what apparatus and equipment to use
- to use simple apparatus and equipment correctly
- to make careful observations and measurements
- to check observations and measurements by repeating them
- to use tables, bar charts and line graphs to present results
- to make comparisons and to identify trends or patterns in results
- to use results to draw conclusions
- to indicate whether the evidence collected supports any prediction made
- to try to explain conclusions in terms of scientific knowledge and understanding

SUPPORTING CURRICULUM LINKS

English	-	Write a job application letter for a job as an astronaut. Give as much useful information about yourself as possible. Describe in detail a journey into space. Write a description of an alien. Write a newspaper report about a UFO landing. Describe an "Earthling" to an alien.
Maths	-	Make a scale drawing showing distances between planets in our solar system.
Geography	-	Research what can be found beneath the earth's surface
History	-	Research the history of space travel.
Technology	-	Design and build an elastic band powered moon buggy.
P.E.	-	Movement - Act out moon walking
R.E.	-	Wonder what may be in the unknown depths of space.

WHOLE CLASS ACTIVITIES

Discuss how shadows are formed and how we can track the movement of the sun by observing shadows.

Discuss how night and day occur due to the earth revolving on its axis.

Discuss the length of time taken for the earth to orbit the sun and the moon to orbit the earth.

Demonstrate the motions of the Earth, Moon and Sun in order to explain day and night and the seasons of the year.

Define gravity and talk about its effects.

Discuss the forces involved.

Define thermal insulation and talk about its uses.

SMALL GROUP ACTIVITIES

Experiment with:
The movement of the sun across the sky.
How day and night are related to the spin of a globe.
Why summer days are longer than winter days.
Why summer is hotter than winter.
Why you can not see the back of the moon.
How different moon shapes are formed.
The effects of gravity on objects.
The forces involved with model parachutes.
The thermal properties of some materials.
Air and water powered model rockets.
Hot air balloons.

STARTING POINTS

Turn the classroom into a space ship/dramatise pupils are space explorers seeking information about a mysterious planet called Earth. Give out "space missions" to accomplish during the duration of the topic.

Assign groups to design and build a scale model planet for use in a classroom solar system.

Discuss where the earth is in relation to the solar system, stars and galaxies.

Recommended Reference Books
First Guide to the Universe - Usborne Books.
Stars and Planets - Usborne Books.
Space - BBC Fact Finders.
Earth and Space - Photocopiable Experiments and Investigations - Topical Resources.

RESOURCES/EQUIPMENT

A collection of reference books; simple scientific apparatus; materials for model making.

Computer program - "Astro" pub by Topologika.

Philip Green A4 Colour Picture Pack - Space.
P.C.E.T. Poster - The Solar System.
The Reluctant Astronomer pack from Molehill Press.

Possible Visits
An observatory or science museum.

Possible Visitors
A scientist from an observatory or a member of a local amateur society of astronauts.

Best Time of Year
Winter - for star gazing at night.

Earth & Space

ART AND DISPLAY

Look at the mood/atmosphere different artists have captured in their paintings of the sky e.g. Turner, Van Gogh.

Paint or draw the landscape near school but put the sky in the style of one of these artists.

Collect pictures of sunsets/storms etc. and use as a stimulus for painting - add an appropriate scene with figures to go with it.

Create in black and white and silver an imaginary lunar landscape - make a junk model of same.

Draw or paint different designs for the sun - look at how other artists and other civilisations have depicted or used the sun in design e.g. Aztecs.

Paint in response to music of Planet Suite Holst.

Draw and describe a new and imaginary planet - or the view from a space ship window (on a circular piece of paper).

INDIVIDUAL ACTIVITIES

Construct your own glossary of astronomical terms e.g. comet, asteroid, milky way, blackhole etc.

Design and make detailed drawings of a space station containing everything you need to survive.

Make a daily record of changes in shape of the moon over one month.

Make a "space race" time-line.

Make a simple model telescope.

Design a space vehicle or moon house.

Make a model lunar landscape with clay model astronauts, model rockets, space station etc.

Design a new type of space suit which provides all the appropriate equipment.

END PRODUCT

Hold a competition for the best model parachute, water powered rocket, elastic band powered lunar-rover etc.

A group talk to the rest of the class complete with one page hand-out describing the investigations made.

Make up individual topic booklets containing reports from experiments, information collected, stories written etc.

A large model moonscape with individual models displayed.

PROGRAMME OF STUDY

Pupils should be taught the way of life, beliefs and achievements of the ancient Greeks and the legacy of ancient Greek civilisation to the modern world:
- Athens and Sparta, e.g. *everyday life, citizens and slaves*
- arts and architecture, e.g. *pottery, sculpture, theatres, temples, public buildings, and how these help us to find out about the ancient Greeks*
- myths and legends of Greek gods and goddesses, heroes and heroines
- relations with other peoples, e.g. *Persians, such as the stories of Marathon, Thermopylae and Salamis, the Greeks in Southern Italy, the campaigns of Alexander the Great, the influences on the Greeks of other civilisations, such as Egypt or Rome*
- influence on the modern world, e.g. *politics, language, sport, architecture, science.*

Pupils should be taught about key features of a past non-European society e.g. Ancient Egypt; this unit should cover:
- key features, including the everyday lives of men and women
- the use of archaeology in finding out about the people and society

SKILLS TO BE DEVELOPED

- to be able to place events, people and changes in periods studied within a chronological framework
- to be able to use dates and terms relating to the passing of time, including ancient, modern, BC, AD, century and decade
- to have an understanding of the characteristic features of particular periods and societies
- to be able to describe and identify reasons for and the results of main events and changes in the periods studied and make links across periods
- to be able to identify and give reasons for different ways in which the past is represented and interpreted
- to be able to find out about aspects of the periods studied from a range of sources of information including documents and printed sources, artefacts, pictures and photographs, music and buildings and sites
- to know the terms necessary to describe the periods and topics studied, including court, monarch, parliament, nation, civilisations, invasion, conquest, settlement, conversion, slavery, trade, industry, law.

SUPPORTING CURRICULUM LINKS

English	-	Debate slavery from the owner/sellers point of view and that of the slave.
Maths	-	Construct model pyramids from nets. Price the seats in a Greek Theatre and work out how much raised from each sitting.
Science	-	Devise a fair test to see how much force is needed to move a house brick on different surfaces.
Technology	-	Make columns out of card and construct a model temple.
Geography	-	Find out which countries border the modern day Egypt and Greece.
P.E.	-	Hold a 'mini' Olympic Games Sports afternoon.
R.E.	-	Listen to the story of Joseph from the Bible.

WHOLE CLASS ACTIVITIES

Collect postcards, photographs, souvenirs from peoples visits to Egypt and Greece in modern times.

Discuss what an "Ancient Civilisation" is and speculate what life would be like before these times.

Make a time line showing some important events in the times of Ancient Greece.

Listen to stories of Athens, Sparta and the Persian wars. Talk about Greek Science, inventions, medicine, astronomy, mathematics and beliefs.

Discuss the meaning of 'Democracy'.

Make a time line showing some important events in the times of Ancient Egypt.

Talk about the nineteenth century excavations of Egyptian graves; how Egyptian society was structured, preservation of bodies and beliefs about the next life etc.

Discuss the importance of the River Nile to Egypt's growth and prosperity.

Learn about the Battle of Kadesh.

SMALL GROUP ACTIVITIES

Map and name cities in the Ancient Greek world.

In small groups produce a short video giving information about one Greek God. Combine with the work of others to make a documentary.

Create a newspaper front page reporting on the Persian wars.

Cook a Greek dish.

Make a group cartoon which illustrates the story 'The Odyssey'.

List similarities/differences shopping now and then.

Experiment with moving heavy blocks on rollers on a level surface and up slopes. Compare with construction of pyramids.

Make a large scale map of Egypt showing the route of the Nile.

Research and write messages in Egyptian hieroglyphics. Make a wall frieze with hieroglyphics around the edges.

STARTING POINTS

Talk about how we know so much about the everyday lives of people who live over 4,000 years ago.

Identify on world maps where Egypt and Greece are to be found.

Estimate using time lines just where in time Ancient Egyptians and Ancients Greeks could be found.

Listen to the story of "The Wooden Horse" and the Sieze of Troy.

Dramatise the story of Pandora's Box.

Introduce the terms A.C. and B.C.

Recommended Reference Books
The Ancient Egyptians Activity Book - British Museum Pub.
Pharaohs and Pyramids - Usborne Books.
Egypt - S & P Harrison - BBC Fact Finders.
The Ancient Greeks Activity Book - British Museum Pub.
Pocket Guide to Ancient Greece - Usborne Books.
The Greeks - Stainer and Sutton - BBC Publications.

RESOURCES/EQUIPMENT

I.T. Arcventure II - The Egyptians.

Videos:
BBC Zig Zag - The Ancient Greeks.
BBC TV - Odyssey.
BBC Landmarks - Egypt.
Philip Green A4 picture packs - Ancient Egypt/Ancient Greece.
Usborne Cut-Out Models - Make this Egyptian Temple.

Possible Visits
Local museum to examine typical items unearthed by an archaeological dig. Exhibitions of Egyptian and Greek artefacts.

Possible Visitors
Museum Curator or Education Officer.
Amateur archaeologist.
A modern Greek/Egyptian man/woman.

Best Time of Year
Any

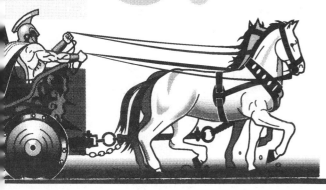

Ancient Civilisations Egypt & Greece

ART AND DISPLAY

Choose an Egyptian or Greek motif and develop in cut paper to become a repeating or border pattern.

Select and use colours from Egyptian or Greek pictures or pottery.

Illustrate a Greek myth or make a 3D or face only character from a Greek myth.

Look at the design of Greek pillars and other Greek architecture - add these characteristics to a house of your own design.

Look at the shape and designs on Greek vases and develop these in clay.

Design your own heiroglyphics and produce a message.

Make a clay model of an Egyptian God.

Compare Greek sculpture/Egyptian portraits then and now.

Design a poster for an Olympic Games.

Make model vases from clay.

Make simple carvings from soap.

INDIVIDUAL ACTIVITIES

Plan a family holiday to Greece within a limited budget.

Make a Greek tunic for a doll.

Make a cut-out model of the Olympic Games.

Read about 'The Minotaurs Maze' and design a maze of your own.

Design a Greek numbers board game.

Write your name in Greek alphabet and send a message to a friend.

Draw a plan of a Greek house.

Draw a Greek trading ship and list its cargo.

Research the work of Archimedes.

Research Egyptian farming, crafts, banquets, games, houses, food, music etc.

Make a model Egyptian funeral boat; copies of Egyptian jewellery; simple house; obelisk etc.

Make crowns for an Egyptian King.

END PRODUCT

Make a large frieze/collage of an Ancient Greek market place or use models to recreate a market place scene.

Create a scene inside an Egyptian Tomb just rediscovered by archaeologists. Recreate as many artefacts as possible e.g. throne, mask, weapons, sandals, wall paintings etc.

Make up individual booklets of children's work including stories written and information collected.

Make a large model of a Trojan Horse.

Use models to recreate the scene of an archaeological dig in the Valley of the Kings.

Act out a typical Greek school day i.e. girls weaving, spinning, cooking etc., boys writing, poetry and doing P.E. Reverse the roles and discuss.

Hold a Greek food tasting session.

Display a frieze of a farmers year.

LIFE PROCESSES AND LIVING THINGS

Work on life processes should be related to pupils' knowledge of animals and plants in the local environment. Work on the variety of life in a habitat should be linked to the reasons for classifying living things.

1. Life processes

Pupils should be taught:

a that there are life processes, including nutrition, movement, growth and reproduction, common to animals, including humans

b that there are life processes, including growth, nutrition and reproduction, common to plants.

2. Humans as organisms

nutrition
a the functions of teeth and the importance of dental care

b that food is needed for activity and for growth, and that an adequate and varied diet is needed to keep healthy

circulation
c a simple model of the structure of the heart and how it acts as a pump

d how blood circulates in the body through arteries and veins

e the effect of exercise and rest on pulse rate

movement
f that humans have skeletons and muscles to support their bodies and to help them to move

growth and reproduction
g the main stages of the human life cycle

health
h that tobacco, alcohol and other drugs can have harmful effects.

3. Green plants as organisms

growth and nutrition
a that plant growth is affected by the availability of light and water, and by temperature

b that plants need light to produce food for growth, and the importance of the leaf in this process

c that the root anchors the plant, and that water and nutrients are taken in through the root and transported through the stem to other parts of the plant

reproduction
d about the life cycle of flowering plants, including pollination, seed production, seed dispersal and germination.

4. Variation and classification

a how locally occurring animals and plants can be identified and assigned to groups, using keys.

5. Living things in their environment

adaptation
a that different plants and animals are found in different habitats

b how animals and plants in two different habitats are suited to their environment

feeding relationships
c that food chains show feeding relationships in an ecosystem

d that nearly all food chains start with a green plant

micro-organisms
e that micro-organisms exist, and that many may be beneficial, e.g. in the breakdown of waste, while others may be harmful, e.g. in causing disease.

COMMENT

Contained on these two pages can be seen the entire content of the Key Stage 2 Programme of Study for Science. At the time of writing, pupils are to be tested towards the end of Year 6 on their retention of content only and not on Experimental and Investigative Science. Some schools choose to visit the Science content twice, firstly in Year 3 or 4 and again in Years 5 and 6. The author believes that this is not strictly necessary, and if there have been taken to make the Science both a thoroughly covered practical and relevant to the age group concerned then much content will be remembered. Consequently to prepare the pupil's for Key Stage 2 Science S.A.T.s teachers need only go through a number of memory jogging exercises. Pupil's performance can be considerably enhanced with only a modest amount of time spent on revision.

REVISION ACTIVITIES

Hold a weekly Science Quiz through out the final year in school.

Go over old S.A.T. papers say twice a week for two terms before the S.A.T.s.

Spend a half term topic unit revisiting the whole Science programme of study. Pupils may like to bring in Science topic booklets they have made earlier. Appropriate videos may be watched. Old test papers could be gone over. A published workbook of test type questions may be worked through.

Alternatives to a half term revision unit could include:
Additional work on Forces and Motion.
Additional work on Materials.
A third habitat studied to supplement work of Life Processes and Living Things.
A repeat of a topic studied in Year 3 in more depth.
A review of the Science topics studied some time previous e.g. topics covered in Years 3 and 4.

MATERIALS AND THEIR PROPERTIES

Work on solids, liquids and gases should be related to pupils' observations of changes that take place when materials are heated and cooled, and to ways in which mixtures can be separated.

Grouping and classifying materials

Pupils should be taught:

a to compare everyday materials, e.g. wood, rock, iron, aluminium, paper, polythene, on the basis of their properties, including hardness, strength, flexibility and magnetic behaviour, and to relate these properties to everyday uses of the materials

b that some materials are better thermal insulators than others

c that some materials are better electrical conductors than others

d to describe and group rocks and soils on the basis of characteristics, including appearance, texture and permeability

e to recognise differences between solids, liquids and gases, in terms of ease of flow and maintenance of shape and volume.

Science S.A.T. Revision Unit

Changing materials

a that mixing materials, e.g. adding salt to water, can cause them to change

b that heating or cooling materials, e.g. water, clay, dough, can cause them to change and that temperature is a measure of how hot or cold they are

c that some changes can be reversed and some cannot

d that dissolving, melting, boiling, condensing, freezing and evaporating are changes that can be reversed

e about the water cycle and the part played by evaporation and condensation

f that the changes that occur when most materials, e.g. wood, wax, natural gas, are burned are not reversible.

Separating mixtures of materials

a that solid particles of different sizes e.g. those in soils, can be separated by sieving

b that some solids, e.g. salt, sugar, dissolve in water to give solutions but some, e.g. sand, chalk, do not

c that insoluble solids can be separated from liquids by filtering

d that solids that have dissolved can be recovered by evaporating the liquid from the solution

e that there is a limit to the mass of solid that can be dissolved in a given amount of water, and that this limit is different for different solids.

PHYSICAL PROCESSES

The relationship between forces and motion should be made clear. It should also be made clear that both light and vibrations from sound sources travel from the sources to a detector. Work on the Earth's place in the solar system should be related to pupils' knowledge about light.

1. Electricity

simple circuits

Pupils should be taught:

a that a complete circuit, including a battery or power supply, is needed to make electrical devices work

b how switches can be used to control electrical devices

c ways of varying the current in a circuit to make bulbs brighter or dimmer

d how to represent series circuits by drawings and diagrams, and how to construct series circuits on the basis of drawings and diagrams.

2. Forces and motion

types of force

a that there are forces of attraction and repulsion between magnets, and forces of attraction between magnets and magnetic materials

b that objects have weight because of the gravitational attraction between them and the Earth

c about friction, including air resistance, as a force which slows moving objects

d that when springs and elastic bands are stretched they exert a force on whatever is stretching them

e that when springs are compressed they exert a force on whatever is compressing them

balanced and unbalanced forces

f that forces act in particular directions

g that forces acting on an object can balance, e.g. in a tug of war, on a floating object, and that when this happens an object at rest stays still

h that unbalanced forces can make things speed up, e.g. an apple being dropped, slow down, e.g. a shoe sliding across the floor, or changing direction, e.g. a ball being hit by a bat.

3. Light and sound

everyday effects of light

a that light travels from a source

b that light cannot pass through some materials, and that this leads to the formation of shadows

c that light is reflected from surfaces, e.g. mirrors, polished metals

seeing

d that we see light sources, e.g. light bulbs, candles, because light from them enters our eyes

vibration and sound

e that sounds are made when objects, e.g. strings on musical instruments, vibrate but that vibrations are not always directly visible

f that the pitch and loudness of sounds produced by some vibrating objects, e.g. a drum skin, a plucked string, can be changed

g that vibrations from sound sources can travel through a variety of materials, e.g. metals, wood, glass, air, to the ear.

4. The Earth and beyond

the Sun, Earth and Moon periodic changes

a that the Sun, Earth and Moon are approximately spherical

b that the position of the Sun appears to change during the day, and how shadows change as this happens

c that the Earth spins around its own axis, and how day and night are related to this spin

d that the Earth orbits the Sun once each year, and that the Moon takes approximately 28 days to orbit the Earth.

PROGRAMME OF STUDY

Investigate family life; groups of people of various combinations that live together and care for each other.

Examine everyday occurences such as how people dress, what they eat, family celebrations such as weddings, birthdays, welcome a new baby, Christmas etc.

Investigate how a Christian family may dress, what they eat, customs and festivals they celebrate and how they worship. Compare with how a Jewish, Sikh, Muslim, Hindu and Buddhist family may do the same. Talk sensitively about why religious families take part in various forms of worship.

SKILLS TO BE DEVELOPED

Study beliefs and practices and relate them to one's own experience.

Enter imaginatively into the motivations, feelings, responses, experiences, hopes, aspirations, beliefs, values, attitudes and perceptions of religious believers.

Think deeply about and question sensitive aspects of human experience.

CURRICULUM LINKS

English	-	Write sensitively about examples of care experienced in your family. Write about care in the community. Discuss how you may react to someone who does not hold the same beliefs as you (religious or otherwise). Debate why you think people hold so many and varied views on religious belief. Think about what you believe it means to hold a faith. Listen to a story from each faith studied.
Science	-	Talk about how scientists believe the world was created. Compare with other views.
Technology	-	Design a small home which can be 'opened up' for a large family occasion.
History	-	Draw a family tree for a fictious Christian family or another family you have researched.
Geography	-	Make a world map showing where religious traditions may have originated.
P.E./Drama	-	Experiment with simple forms of meditation.

WHOLE CLASS ACTIVITIES

Make up a fictitious group of people to represent a Christian family. Given them names and characters.

Talk about how the family would dress. Sketch items of clothing or make collections from old catalogues. Do the same for food.

Discuss in detail the events that may take place at a Christening and a Wedding Celebration.

Talk about a Christmas celebration and what it means to a Christian family.

Study in detail Sunday worship, the form it takes, the taking of break and wine and what the ritual represents. Think carefully about how the members of your fictitious Christian family would feel during each of these occasions.

SMALL GROUP ACTIVITIES

In a small group research how a family from another faith may live.

Find out appropriate names; everyday dress and dress for special occasions; everyday food and food for festivals; examples of customs and celebrations the family may participate in and some examples of worship. Collect pictures and artifacts. Construct, practice and finally make a group presentation to the rest of the class demonstrating information collected.

Make a collage/frieze which depicts care in a family.

Devise a new "Grace" a Christian family may use before a meal.

STARTING POINTS

Talk about the make-up of a family, which may include one or two parents, grand-parents etc.

Discuss the ways they show care for each other.

Talk about special events that are common to family groups e.g. a birth ceremony, a wedding, a birthday, Christmas time etc. What special things happen at these times to the family group.

Recommended Reference Books

I am a Jew; I am a Sikh; I am a Muslim; I am a Hindu; I am a Buddhist; I am a Roman Catholic - Pub. by Franklin Watts.
Westhill Project - Christians 1 & 2 - Read, Rudge and Howarth - Pub. M.G.P.

RESOURCES/EQUIPMENT

Dictionary; Encyclopedia; School Library; Slides; Videos; Posters etc.

A good collection of children's reference works which touch on the theme.

Pictures of worship and family life from different religious traditions, e.g. P.C.E.T. wallcharts "My Religion", "Rites of Passage", "Festivals" etc. Example of artefacts used in worship available from 'Articles of Faith Ltd', King Street, Bury, Lancs or The Festival Shop, Kings Heath, Birmingham.

Possible Visits
If possible, visit the home of someone from a different culture of your own.

Possible Visitors
A member of a religious family to talk about celebration of special family events.

Living in a Faith

ART AND DISPLAY

For different faiths collect pictures of: symbols, festivals, food, costumes, places of worship etc. Use these as a stimulus for drawing and painting.

Collect artefacts from different faiths making sure they are handled sensitively and appropriately. Use these for observational drawing.

Paint pictures which depict milestones in the Christian faith such as Baptism/Confirmation etc.

Make drawings/designs for an event e.g. a christening robe or a wedding dress.

Look at cards which depict special occasions in the church year and produce a design of your own.

Illustrate a favourite Bible story. Look at books from other faiths and illustrate stories.

INDIVIDUAL ACTIVITIES

Make a simple chart and record facts about Christian, Jewish, Sikh, Muslim, Hindu and Buddhist food, dress, customs, worship etc.

Research a menu and shopping list for a vegetarian meal.

Draw and sketch artifacts of worship from pictures and slides.

Copy out the Sikh alphabet.

Make pictures of a wedding celebration from two different faiths.

END PRODUCT

Display of written and creative work or individual booklets made.

Plan and cook a vegetarian meal for pupils to sample.

Make a collage for each of the six major world faiths depicting scenes from family life.

Hold a class assembly which tells of family life in different religious traditions.

Make a large frieze of "Faith is ...." poems.

PROGRAMME OF STUDY

Pupils should be taught about the lives of men, women and children at different levels of society in Britain and the ways in which they were affected by the Second World War and changes in technology and transport:

- changes in industry and transport, including the impact of new technologies, e.g. *motor cars, computers, space travel*
- the impact of the Second World War on the people of Britain, e.g. *evacuation, the Blitz, the armed forces, rationing*
- at home, e.g. *family life at different levels of society, housing conditions, diet and health, changes in the roles of men and women*
- at work, e.g. *the Depression, changes in employment, automation, men and women at work, emigration and immigration*
- at leisure, e.g. *radio, cinema and television, the Festival of Britain, sport, holidays.*

SKILLS TO BE DEVELOPED

- to be able to place events, people and changes in periods studied within a chronological framework
- to be able to use dates and terms relating to the passing of time, including ancient, modern, BC, AD, century and decade
- to have an understanding of the characteristic features of particular periods and societies
- to be able to describe and identify reasons for and the results of main events and changes in the periods studied and make links across periods
- to be able to identify and give reasons for different ways in which the past is represented and interpreted
- to be able to find out about aspects of the periods studied from a range of sources of information including documents and printed sources, artefacts, pictures and photographs, music and buildings and sites
- to know the terms necessary to describe the periods and topics studied, including court, monarch, parliament, nation, civilisations, invasion, conquest, settlement, conversion, slavery, trade, industry, law.

SUPPORTING CURRICULUM LINKS

English	-	Interview people in each of six decades about types of work done and working conditions. Debate the possible causes of the changes found.
Maths	-	Carry out simple calculations using pounds, shillings and pence. Compare imperial and metric weights.
Science	-	Compose a typical war time menu and test classroom reaction to contents.
Technology	-	Design and construct a model prefabricated house which can easily be assembled on a new site.
Geography	-	Make a map of the countries invaded by Germany during the Second World War.
Music	-	Hold a "Juke Box Jury" type quiz show and evaluate examples of popular music from different decades.
R.E.	-	Discuss feelings of bereavement felt by a family on receipt of a "killed in action" telegram.

WHOLE CLASS ACTIVITIES

Talk about oral history and how we can find out about the recent past by talking to people around us.

Talk about local history and how our community is part of the wider world and was affected by important events such as World War II.

Talk about different interpretations of similar events.

Devise appropriate questions to ask someone who was a teenager/young person during the 30's; 40's; 50's; 60's; 70's; 80's etc. Test your questions on friends. Consider arrangements e.g. meeting place; how to make a person relax; being sensitive etc. Carry out a number of interviews (at least two different people for each period in time).

Talk about and collect other examples of recent local historical evidence e.g. old photographs, old newspapers, household objects, musical recordings, personal letters etc.

Visit houses in the area that have been built in the last sixty years. List similarities and differences.

SMALL GROUP ACTIVITIES

Listen to oral history tapes from one period. Examine for different points of view. Speculate how these may occur. Research which is probably most accurate.

Listen to two different accounts of one specific event. Construct a newspaper report from the information.

Edit one or two interviews using two tape-recorders. Add your own commentary to make an interesting item for a local radio station.

Edit a tape. Collect war time pictures and artifacts etc. Use tape and collection to make an interesting corner in an exhibition.

Examine war time photographs. Use tape recorders to create a short story complete with sound effects for a radio station.

STARTING POINTS

Make a time-line of new inventions which have come into use over the last sixty years e.g. computers, space craft, jet planes, etc. Discuss how this could change peoples lives.

Write to/make a programme/visit a local radio station to let local people know of your study and appeal for artefacts or documents which tell of local happenings over the last sixty years.

Listen to a class novel set around the time of the Second World War e.g. "The Silver Sword" by Ian Serraillier pub. by Puffin Books or "Carrie's War" by Nina Bawden - Pub. by Puffin.

Watch the I.T.V. series 'How We Used to Live'.

Recommended Reference Books
The Twentieth Century - R.S. Unstead - Pub. by A & C Black.
Into Modern Times 1901-1945 - T. Wood - Pub. by Paperbird (Ladybird).
How We Used to Live 1936-1953 by F Kelsall - Pub. by Simon and Schuster.

RESOURCES/EQUIPMENT

A tape recorder and microphone.
How We Used to Live - 1936-1953 - a Yorkshire Television Series.
Reproduction newspapers depicting important events.
Collection of popular music from different decades.
A collection of World War II postcards/cuttings/artefacts.
Archive wartime sound recordings.

Possible Visits
Old people's home to interview some of the residents.
A local antique shop.
A local museum to examine artefacts.
Local reference library or newspaper office.

Possible Visitors
A parent/friend who was a teenager in the 1930's; 1940's; 1950's; 1960's; 1970's; 1980's.
A parent/friend prepared to talk about World War experiences. Someone who has emigrated to another country. Someone who has immigrated to our country.

Best Time of Year
Any.

Local history study of
Britain
Since 1930

ART AND DISPLAY

Transport - housing - clothes - occupations - pastimes (then and now) make drawings and paintings of actual objects or from photographs.

A comic strip style of important events from 1930 onwards.

A collage of events of each decade.

Buildings in the locality since 1930 - photographs how it was - models of then and now.

Employment then and now. Design a poster to advertise jobs/rates of pay then and now.

The oldest and newest building in the locality.

INDIVIDUAL ACTIVITIES

Devise a questionnaire to give to members of your family of various ages. Ask about school, home comforts and entertainment. Compare the outcome with the present day.

Research orally people's experiences of changes in transport, dress, diet, cinema, radio and television etc.

Make individual collage pictures to be included in a Time-Line of fashion.

Make models/pictures of planes, ships and cars showing changes through the decades.

Make model houses to be used in class street scene.

Paint replica coronation souvenirs.

Make sketches showing the changes in a person from 1930 to 1990.

END PRODUCT

A large time line across the classroom/school hall/entrance displaying events in each decade complete with illustrations and evidence to support the facts.

A radio or T.V. programme that tells about life in one decade or across the last six decades.

A display of one particular event such as V.E. Day or the Festival of Britain.

Make a display of children's books or play things over the last sixty years.

Make a local history museum and ask O.A.P.'s/older members of the community to visit.

Make a mock up of the inside of a wartime shelter or some other period scene.

RESEARCH SKILLS	Nursery/Reception	Years 1 & 2
To be developed in all topics	The child should be able to:	The child should be able to:
OBSERVATION	- make observsations first hand from a variety of objects, displays, pictures, walks etc. with some guidance as to what to look for.	- collect information by looking at pictures, simple reference books, objects, displays etc.
REFERENCING	- recognise that print is used to carry meaning. - talk about the content of an illustrated non-fiction book. - ask questions.	- read and understand straight forward signs, labels and notices. - demonstrate knowledge of the alphabet in using word books and simple dictionaries. - find the right page in a book. - ask questions of older people.
SPEAKING & LISTENING	- participate in group activities - participate in imaginative play - listen and respond to stories and poems. - follow instructions	- participate as speakers and listeners in a group. -describe an event - listen attentively to stories and poems. - listen, talk and ask questions with the teacher. - follow instructions.
WRITING/ RECORDING	- use pictures, symbols or isolated letters, words or phrases. - to communicate meaning. - draw pictures - make simple models.	- write simple sentences independently. - draw pictures -draw plans and diagrams. - make picture graphs. - make simple models.
INTERPRETING INFORMATION	- talk about pictures, objects, displays, books, etc. - talk about simple maps and picture charts.	- describe the main features in a picture or objects. - interpret picture maps, picture graphs and simple plans.
PREDICTING & HYPOTHESISING	- talk about "what may happen next" during story time.	- make simple predictions following observations. eg. what could happen next?

Years 3 & 4	Years 5 & 6
The child should be able to:	The child should be able to:
- collect information from a wide variety of sources:objects, pictures books, filmstrips, slides etc.	- select appropriate information from a wide variety of sources: objects, pictures, books, maps, filmstrips, slides etc.
- collect information from books and other sources. - choose a suitable book from a number of books. - use a contents page.	- select relevant information from books and other source. - use an index. - use the reference section in a library. - use an encyclopaedia.
- give an account of observations and experiences. - speak in front of others. - contribute to a joint discussion. - question. - listen. - follow instructions.	- be fluent in describing and recounting. - give an account in a logical sequence. - make relevant comments. - discuss and present a reasoned argument. - question and draw conclusions. - listen. - follow instructions.
- write an account of observations and experiences - make visual representations. - make block graphs, charts and diagrams - make models. - present neat, well set out work.	- write an account of logical sequence. - present a reasoned argument. - present neat, well organised written work. -choose the most appropriate method of recording and illustrating work. - work with other children to produce a group study. - use tables, charts, diagrams, graphs, drawings and models to supplement written work.
- interpret maps, plans, diagrams, tables, charts etc. - analyse information at a simple level (answering simple questions; what does it mean? Why?). synthesise information (use several sources to obtain information e.g. a picture and a map.	- interpret information from several sources. - recognise that there is more than one point of view. - notice inconsistinces. - make judgement about authors, dates of publication assessing fact and opinion, accuracy of source, relevance of information gathered. - make generalisations; offer alternative explanations. - synthesise information; producing coherence from several sources. - draw conclusions.
- make predictions - make guesses about causes.	- make predictions. - attempt to explain causes and effects. - plan the next stage in own research.

SELECTED BIBLIOGRAPHY

Early Years

Tina Bruce (1987) Early Childhood Education - Hodder and Stoughton.
D Fontana (1984) The Education of Young Children - Blackwell.
The Early Admission to School of Four Year Old Children (1987) Lancashire County Council.
G Barrett (1986) Starting School: An Evaluation of the Experience A.M.M.A
P P Lillard (1972) Montessori - A Modern Approach - Schocken Books - New York.
K Manning & A Sharpe (1977) Structuring Play in the Early Years at School - Ward Lock.
Mollie Jenkins (1973) School Without Tears - Collins.

Topic/Project/Thematic Work in General

Jan Stewart (1986) The Making of the Primary School - Croom Helm, London.
P Rance (1968) Teaching by Topics - Ward Lock Educational.
D Wray (1987) Teaching Information Skills through Project Work.
Bradley/Eggleston/Kerry/Cooper (1985) Developing Pupils Thinking Through Topic Work: A Starter Course - Longman for S.C.D.C.
R Lane (1981) Project Work in the Primary School - Preston C.D.C.
P Bell (1985) History, Geography, Science, Nature and R.E. Primary School Topics - A Skills Approach - Preston C.D.C.
J Makoff L Duncan (1986) Display for all seasons. A thematic approach to Infant Teaching - Belair Publications Ltd.
H Pluckrose (1987) What is Happening in our Primary Schools.

Subject Disciplines

J Blyth (1988) History 5 - 9 -Hodder and Stoughton.
Geography from 5 to 16. Curriculum Matters 7. (1986) H.M.S.O.
Lancashire Looks at.... Science in the Early Years (1986) Lancashire County Council.
Discovering an Approach. Religious Education in Primary Schools, (1977) Macmillan Education for Schools Council.
G Read, J Rudge, R B Howarth (1987) The Westhill Project R.E. 5 - 16 Mary Glasgow Publications Ltd.
Design and Primary Education (1987) The Design Council.

National Curriculum

English in the National Curriculum - D.E.S. -Pub H.M.S.O.
Mathematics in the National Curriculum - D.E.S. - Pub H.M.S.O.
Science in the National Curriculum - D.E.S. - Pub H.M.S.O.
Technology in the National Curriculum - D.E.S. - Pub H.M.S.O.
History in the National Curriculum - D.E.S. - Pub H.M.S.O.
Geography in the National Curriculum - D.E.S. - Pub H.M.S.O.
Aspects of Primary Education:
The Teaching and Learning of Science - H.M.I.
The Teaching and Learning of History and Geography - H.M.I.
The Education of Children Under Five - H.M.I.